P9-BIS-462

Beer Making for All

Also by James Macgregor

WINE MAKING FOR ALL

BEER MAKING FOR ALL

JAMES MACGREGOR

FABER & FABER LTD
London

First published in 1967
by Faber and Faber Limited
24 Russell Square London WC1
Reprinted 1968, 1970
Printed in Great Britain by
Latimer Trend & Co Ltd Whitstable
All rights reserved

ISBN O 571 08220 3

© *James Macgregor 1967*

Contents

Introduction

Hermit hoar, in solemn cell,
Wearing out life's evening gray;
Strike thy bosom, sage! and tell
What is bliss, and which the way?
Thus I spoke, and speaking sighed,
Scarce repressed the starting tear,
When the hoary sage replied,
'Come, my lad, and drink some beer.'
Anecdotes of Johnson
by MRS. PIOZZI

Spirits are strongest, wine is most seductive, but *beer is best*.

That's only an opinion, of course, and not necessarily mine. Yet what else can you drink for the whole of a convivial evening, and not end up under the table? Some say tea; but this is a frivolous answer. Coffee, it is well known, is a dangerous drug. Water is for men dying of thirst in Death Valley. Just imagine an apparently normal, healthy person sitting in a corner at a party drinking pint after pint of cool, clear water. Any observer with the slightest scientific curiosity would be bound to wonder what was wrong with him. Had he taken a religious vow, was he doing it for a bet, or was the poor chap suffering from diabetes?

INTRODUCTION

Beer is the drink of The People. That gives it tremendous snob value in a democracy. The person who drinks Chablis with rump steak or Sauternes before the meal even starts is shrivelled to a cringing husk by the unanimous scorn of those who think they know better. But you can't go wrong with beer. A beer drinker can't be insulted—he's too ignorant.

Beer has, arguably, a longer history than either wine or spirits. Whisky, brandy, rum, vodka, gin and other explosively potent drinks cannot be produced without distillation, a process beyond genuine primitives. But primitives always manage to produce some kind of beer. They make beer first, then wine, then spirits.

Beer is a happy drink. It's true that there are beer rowdies and beer melancholics. These are unfortunate people who, when they are spiritually and emotionally released, can do no more than demonstrate conclusively that they ought to have remained shut up. On the whole, however, beer makes people inoffensively happy, reluctant to move except eventually to bed, to sleep, perchance to snore.

There is only one thing that can fairly be said against beer, except by teetotallers and other masochists, and that is that it is ruinously expensive. Half a crown for a pint is a criminal toll on one of the essentials of life. But this is a free country (since 1963). We don't have to pay 2s. 6d., or the greater part thereof, for a pint. We can make it ourselves for about threepence.

If we do, we can really afford to drink beer. And we can still be snobs if we like. If one can be a snob over not having TV or a car, one can certainly be a snob over drinking beer at 3d. a pint instead of 2s. 6d.

All the best people do it . . . or would if they had the savvy.

10

INTRODUCTION

The economic barrier having been annihilated, there remain other possible snags which any sensible person should consider. Is beer making messy, smelly, arduous, time-consuming, and do you have to be an expert before you can guarantee that every second brew won't have to be poured down the sink? The answer in each case is the same: beer making can be all things to all men (and women too). If you are allergic to mess, you adopt a technique which may involve a little more trouble, a little more time and possibly more expense, but which will be as clinically unmessy as anyone could wish. If time and trouble are the principal things you can't afford, there are methods of making beer with so little effort that by far the most arduous and time-consuming stage in the whole operation is the stage of drinking the beer. If you don't want to become an expert, there's no real need. You follow one of the simplest methods blindly, rigidly, every time, and your beer always turns out exactly the same.

The one snag that remains is smell. It must be admitted that certain odours, not all of them comparable to Chanel No. 5, inevitably occur in beer making. But one must remember that beer itself, the finished product, does not provide one of the most serenely fragrant olfactory experiences the world has to offer. Connoisseurs praise or condemn the bouquet of a wine, but literature is strangely lacking in lyrical eulogy of the smell of beer. You drink it, you don't smell it. Much the same applies in beer making. You make it, you don't smell it. There are ways, however, in which the fastidious beer maker, if such a creature exists, can reduce this assault on his sensibilities to a minimum, even without recourse to a clothespin.

This is not a book for the scientific beer maker. If he wants

11

to know exactly what chromatographic methods have established about the changes during malting of the carbohydrates and proteins of the barley grains, he will have to seek enlightenment elsewhere. If he wants to know all about the humulone, cohumulone and adhumulone, plus prehumulone and posthumulone, which are the principal compounds in the α-acid of the hop cone . . . well, jolly good luck to him.

It is not a book for the recipe collector. Any practical beer maker should know enough about the basic materials and methods to be able to prepare a beer very much as a housewife prepares a cup of tea. Experience is necessary in the selection of the tea, in the quantity used, the manner of infusion, and the quantities of milk and sugar added. Such experience is easily and painlessly acquired. It is almost as easy to vary intelligently, predictably and successfully the type of beer which will result as it is, without having to taste at every stage, to make a strong, sweet cup of Indian tea or a pale, delicate, lemon-flavoured China.

It is because the home brewer should know what he is doing rather than exactly how to do it that detailed descriptions of methods come very late in this book—and are not tremendously detailed when they do appear. If in general you understand how beer is made, what is essential in the brewing process and what is optional, the details can't trip you up. You can invent your own methods and recipes. Every successful brewer does.

Come, my lad, and make some beer.

CHAPTER I

The Easy Way

Water is best.
PINDAR

Of course water is best. Without it, you can't make anything else.

Chemically, making beer is an extremely complicated business. Fortunately, it's not in the least necessary to be able to give a scientific lecture on what you're doing to be able to do it quite successfully. Otherwise none of us would be able to switch on television.

It is now possible to buy a tin of instant beer, or more accurately, instant wort, for 5s. Wort is the word used for the liquid which is to become beer. All you have to do with this instant wort is pour it in a plastic bucket, add boiling water, stir, add yeast when cool and cover the bucket. Bottle a week later and drink the beer a week after that.

Beer made this way is excellent. (I'm drinking some of it now.)

Why bother, then, to make beer by longer and more complicated methods?

There's always a great deal to be gained by that extra touch, as long as it's not one touch too many. A three-course lunch *could* be supplied in a single tin, merely to be tipped out and heated—soup, vegetables, meat, sauce, apple tart, coffee, cheese and biscuits all mixed together. Why this idea hasn't caught on is too obvious to require explanation.

If we do use one of the instant worts obtainable from suppliers of materials for beer making, it is advisable to take a little more trouble than the summary above demands— perhaps more than the instructions supplied suggest.

Any such prepared wort will consist of malt extract flavoured with hops. Other flavourings may have been added, and the instructions should be followed closely the first time. These flavoured malt extracts should not be confused with the made-up packets of malt and hops to make a specified quantity of beer. We'll come to them later.

Here is a more detailed summary of what should be done with a 2-lb. tin of instant wort.

Pour the extract into a clean plastic bucket which has a lid. Heating the tin previously in hot water will make it pour more easily. Pour some boiling water in the bucket and some in the tin. Hot water will enable you to get all the extract from the tin into the bucket. Stir and make up the total to two gallons for a fairly strong beer, or three gallons for a weaker beer. Replace the bucket lid. When the extract is all dissolved in the water and the liquid is quite cool, add a bottom-working ale or beer yeast, obtained at the same time and from the same supplier as the instant wort, and replace the lid again.

When the beer will be ready for bottling depends on the temperature in which the bucket is kept. It could be as little as four days in summer; it could be more than fourteen days in winter. Wait until the bubbling in the bucket has almost ceased and then pour the beer very carefully into a similar bucket, leaving an inch or two of residue in the first bucket. The pouring must be steady and complete in a single operation, so that the sediment is undisturbed and remains in the first bucket. Throw this sediment away.

Bottle the beer. Use strong screwtop bottles and stand them upright. In one to three weeks the bottles will pop when unscrewed, and clear beer with a good head can be poured without sediment if the glass is tilted, the pouring is done in one steady motion, and the last inch or so is left in the bottle.

Well, that's certainly not difficult. All you need is:

A plastic bucket with a lid, capacity at least three gallons.

Another clean container which holds about the same quantity.

A 2-lb. tin of instant wort (hop-flavoured malt extract).

Screwtop bottles (16 pint bottles for two gallons, 24 for three).

Bottom-working beer yeast.

You can also make five gallons using a 2-lb tin of instant wort plus two to three pounds of sugar. The method is exactly the same except that you need a five-gallon plastic container and the sugar is dissolved with the extract in boiling water, making a total of five gallons.

It must be emphasized that special *hop-flavoured* malt extract has to be obtained. Ordinary malt extract, easily obtainable from any chemist, won't do, unless hops or hop extract are added.

It is quite possible to go on making beer in this way, with or without sugar, and never wish to know more or make a different kind of beer. Most people, however, are impelled by curiosity, if nothing else, to find out more, and by a desire for variety to try producing different kinds of beer.

All commercial types of beer can be imitated. To try to duplicate a named beer is neither desirable nor necessary, although by trial and error it could probably be done quite successfully. The home brewer's aim is rather to produce a range of weak and strong beers, pale ales and dark ales, mild and bitter beers, lagers and stouts.

All these are beers. Originally ale was unhopped beer, but now all so-called ale is hopped. Every beer, and that includes all ales, lagers and stouts, is made from malt in some form and hops in some form, with or without the addition of sugar, other grain such as barley, rice, maize, bran or wheat, and possibly flavouring other than hops.

If you want to make a range of beers, you must know more and do more than the instant wort method requires. Different malts must be used. There are many types, the most important being pale, crystal, amber, chocolate and black. Home brew suppliers list only pale, crystal, black and patent black. You may have to vary the nature of your water, soften hard water or harden soft water. You may have to use sugar other than the ordinary household kind. Extras like liquorice, caramel, treacle, golden syrup, citric acid and salt may be needed.

The use of hop-flavoured malt extract is undeniably the simplest way there is; every other technique demands more know-how and involves more work.

First it is necessary to know certain things about yeast. Without yeast fermentation is impossible. Without fermentation, alcohol is impossible. Before you can have beer, ale, stout, red wine, white wine, champagne, sherry, port, whisky, rum, vodka, brandy, gin or any of the liqueurs, there must be yeast and there must be fermentation.

Yeast is a living, indeed aggressive organism which has the property of being able to split sugar into alcohol and carbon dioxide. The world already has plenty of carbon dioxide and is not particularly interested in the production of more. Consequently in all fermentation (the process of yeast working on sugar), the carbon dioxide is thrown away as waste. But the alcohol is carefully preserved in the liquid.

Fermentation, although a natural process, seldom occurs in nature—or rather, when it does it doesn't stop in time to produce drinkable alcohol. There is a further stage which beer and wine makers have to prevent. The alcohol produced by yeast in a sugary liquid will turn into acetic acid (vinegar) if not protected from certain bacteria always to be found in the air. Consequently no fermenting liquid should ever be left uncovered for more than a few minutes at a time, and it is even more important that once fermentation is over the air should not get at the liquid. Once beer or wine has turned to acetic acid, there is no way to reverse the process.

In beer making there isn't much danger of such a disaster. Every beer drinker knows that beer of any kind, once poured, must be drunk within a fairly short time or it will go flat, stale, insipid. So there's no need to tell a beer drinker that beer can't be stored in open jugs, casks or buckets. He already knows. As a matter of fact, beer left in a tankard for two or three hours and then declared undrinkable *hasn't* suffered bacterial spoilage. It has not become vinegar. There hasn't been time. It has merely lost all its gas, and possibly become hazy through the formation of large molecules of protein, carbohydrates and metal ions. But there is general agreement that beer must be gassy. Without that familiar tingle of carbon dioxide on tongue and palate, beer becomes rather nasty stuff.

Spoilage seldom occurs in beer fermenting in a bucket with only a loose lid over it, because the fermentation is so rapid and vigorous. Every second thousands of tiny bubbles of carbon dioxide are rising to the surface of the liquid and bursting there, forming a thick, creamy foam or head. Though less dense than the liquid, carbon dioxide is heavier than air. It therefore lies thickly on the surface of the liquid and forms a protective blanket.

Earlier it was stated that in fermentation carbon dioxide is ejected as waste. This is true—in fermentation. After fermentation, however, some has to be preserved. Beer is bottled at a stage when nearly all the sugar has been converted to carbon dioxide and alcohol, and nearly all the yeast has settled to the bottom and can be left behind by careful pouring. But some sugar remains, and some yeast gets into the bottle. This yeast again gets to work, producing more alcohol and more carbon dioxide. Now, however, the gas is trapped. That's why screwtop bottles are essential. Corks, unless wired down like champagne corks, are quite useless. Some two weeks later, when the bottle is opened, the beer is carbonated like aerated waters, naturally conditioned for drinking. And since by this time the yeast has again settled to the bottom, the beer can be poured off with very little yeast in it.

Another simple way of making beer, although not quite as simple as the instant wort method, is by the use of packets of malt and hops obtainable from specialist suppliers. These are very cheap, working out at about a shilling a gallon. If anything but a very weak beer or stout is made from these packets, however, sugar must be added, taking the cost up to about two shillings a gallon.

The packets come with simple instructions. The mixed malt (grain) and hops (dried and flaky, like leaves pressed in a book) are boiled for an hour or more, the strained liquor is poured over sugar, and when the quantity has been made up with water and the wort is cool, yeast is added. From then on the process is exactly the same as with instant wort.

This is quite simple, too, but for two reasons the beer is not as good as that properly made from instant wort. The first is that simple boiling is a compromise, recommended only because proper brewing methods are too complicated to explain on a label, to be carried out by someone who may be making beer for the first time in total ignorance of brewing procedure. The second is that the supplier, naturally enough, has made up a weak, cheap, simple mixture, not to be compared with beer made from more generous quantities of malt and hops.

You may have no intention of making wine, and you can't make spirits anyway, not if you propose to stay out of jail. Nevertheless, understanding what is common to the production of all alcoholic drinks helps the beer maker to avoid pitfalls.

Beer is fermented from a sugary liquid extracted from malt and flavoured with hops. Wine is fermented from a sugary liquid, the juice of grapes, and normally is not flavoured. Country wines made by amateurs are made from a sugary liquid obtained from fruit, vegetables, cereals or flowers, also usually unflavoured. Sherry and port are ordinary wines fortified by the addition of spirits. Liqueurs are wines, usually fortified with spirits, and flavoured with herbs, etc. Spirits are wines and ales which have been taken a stage further by distillation.

Now let's have a look at the differences.

First, different yeasts are used. Earlier I ducked the question of yeast varieties by simply specifying a bottom-working beer yeast for home beer making. In fact, top-working yeast is very largely used in breweries. Instead of falling to the bottom, this yeast rises to the top and does its work there. When the brewer wants to get rid of it, he skims it off with a great moving blade like a snowplough.

Bottom-working yeast is used in wine making, but it's not the same as a beer yeast. It works more slowly, for a longer time, and has to be capable of fermenting to a greater alcohol percentage than a beer yeast.

The main difference between making wine at home and making beer is that wine has to be protected far more. You can start wine in a bucket (the initial extract is called must instead of wort), but after a few days you have to put it in casks or jars fitted with an airlock which lets gas out and prevents air entering. Failure to do this would mean that during the long, slow fermentation, possibly taking the best part of a year before it could really be considered complete, the wine would almost certainly succumb to vinegar bacteria and be spoiled.

Beer has more in common with champagne than with ordinary wine, which is quite still. Indeed, any frothing in wine after it is uncorked, sometimes encountered in cheap Spanish wines, indicates that the wine has not been sufficiently matured, and the bottle should be taken straight back to the wine merchant, who, if he is not a rogue, will be glad to replace the bottle and much concerned over the condition of the rest of his supplies.

Champagne in the early stages of its production is an ordinary wine (except that it is a white wine produced from black grapes). But then something happens which is similar to beer practice. The wine is primed with fresh juice and firmly stoppered, so that further fermentation takes place in the bottle, more alcohol and carbon dioxide are formed, the gas cannot escape and the wine become sparkling. What happens after that is different from home beer making but similar to commercial brewing practice—the yeast is removed without allowing the gas to escape, the bottle is firmly stoppered, and when the cork is eventually removed, the wine is sparkling yet without sediment.

In case anyone thinks of trying it—it really is barely possible for the beer maker to have sparkle in his beer and no sediment at all.

Champagne apart, wine is deliberately made as still and stable as possible, and consequently *all* the yeast has to be removed before bottling. This is done principally by many rackings. Racking is the process of drawing off wine (or beer) without disturbing the sediment.

The important point here is that the beer maker, unlike the wine maker, must make sure he never entirely eliminates the yeast. If he did, the beer would be permanently flat beyond possibility of sparkle. Thus, while in wine making it seldom matters much if a particular racking is delayed for a month or so, beer made at home is usually racked once or at most twice, and at a carefully-chosen stage when fermentation is nearly but not quite over.

*   *   *

THE EASY WAY

So far the only brewing methods which have been considered are elementary. In contrast, the methods of the professionals, the commercial brewers, are now briefly described.

Anyone who is daunted by the immense complication and commercialization of modern brewing methods should remember instant wort. Although it's not as instantaneous as all that, anyone who wants to make beer by a still simpler method must be like the amateur scientist who had his house rigged up so that doors opened automatically whenever he whistled a certain note. This wasn't good enough, however. He went back to his laboratory and devised a new system—so that he could dispense with the whistle.

CHAPTER II

The Hard Way

How the professionals do it

I feel no pain, dear mother, now
But oh! I am so dry!
Oh, take me to a brewery
And leave me there to die.

SHANTY

The United States and Britain have been described as two countries divided by a common language. It's equally true that commercial and home brewing are two similar processes which couldn't be more different.

It should be made clear at the outset, however, that one is not better than the other. A figure painstakingly carved out of wood is not necessarily better or worse than two million plastic figures produced in a factory from the same mould.

If the beer we bought at the local were made exactly as home brewers make it, in home-brewing quantities, it would not cost 3d.–6d. a pint. It would cost, probably, at least 9s. a pint. We don't have to pay for our own labour. We should certainly have to pay for somebody else's.

Commercial methods are aimed at producing, in quantity,

beer of a uniform standard, strength and taste. When we buy any proprietary brand, we don't have to wonder: 'What will it taste like this time?' We ask for a particular beer because we already know how it will taste.

Draught beer used to be delivered to hotels and public-houses in large wooden casks. As a cask is emptied, the nature of the pint drawn for the customer changes, if only slightly. In the bad old days not so long ago, murky pints, flat pints, stale pints and metal-contaminated pints were pushed casually across the bar counter, and complaints were met not so much with indifference as with honest puzzlement. Draught beer was like that, wasn't it? If you wanted a brilliant beer with a creamy head, why didn't you ask for a bottled beer?

Draught beers in kegs, usually of stainless steel, have been introduced to provide brilliance and an unchanging standard of quality, condition and flavour, with considerable success.

The brewer wants you to drink his beer in the best possible condition. Consequently commercial brewing is becoming more and more scientific. Malt and hops are analysed in the laboratory with the object of ensuring uniformity.

As in other commercial enterprises, no successful product is changed while it continues to be successful unless the change is obviously and undeniably for the better. When a new beer is announced with triumphant heraldry, and an old beer is quietly withdrawn, it's usually because sales have been falling.

Briefly, the main stages in brewing are:
    Conversion of barley to malt.
    Crushing of malt in mills to grist.
    Mashing in hot water.

Draining of wort, sparging.
Boiling with hops.
Cooling.
Yeasting and fermentation.
Settling, priming and fining.
Racking.
Storing in casks or bottling.

In more detail:

Conversion of barley to malt: The starch in barley is not fermentable, but the starch in malt can be turned into sugar and dextrin by steeping in hot water (mashing). Not only barley can be malted. But barley is so superior to other grains for the purpose that only in a barley famine would major efforts to find a substitute be necessary.

First the barley is cleaned, or screened. Then it is steeped in water for three days, the water being changed several times. The grains swell and become soft. Then the barley is placed on a malting floor, warm, dark, dry and well ventilated. The grain begins to germinate, and a shoot begins to grow. The grains are regularly raked and turned over so that germination is uniform.

After three or four days the malt is dried and heated in a kiln to halt growth. The temperature is of vital importance in producing different types of malt. Pale and crystal malts are not heated beyond 85° C, but dark malts are roasted at over 100° C.

Crushing of malt in mills to grist: The malt is passed between rollers which grind it lightly, not to powder.

Mashing in hot water: This, the process of extracting solids from the malt into a fermentable liquid, was probably done for thousands of years, quite effectively too, before anybody had the faintest idea what, chemically, was happening. It must have been found out, by trial and error, that cold water didn't work, and boiling water didn't work. If the water wasn't at just the right temperature, the beer turned out weak and miserable. It was also discovered that at the right temperature, about 65° C, too short mashing was ineffective and over-long immersion accomplished nothing more than two or three hours' mashing did.

We now know what goes on: at the right temperature, 65° C, the enzyme diastase turns the starch into malt sugar (maltose) and dextrin. An enzyme has the property of being able to split compounds into simpler substances. And diastase, as well as other necessary enzymes, is formed during the malting process. Thus if we were using plain barley for mashing instead of malt, there would be little or none of the required enzyme activity, the starch wouldn't be converted, couldn't ferment subsequently, and the result would be a thin barley beer, alcoholic but only just.

Malt, on the other hand, has enough diastase to convert more than the starch already present, and it is therefore possible and economically sound to add to the mash un-malted barley, maize, oatmeal, wheat or rice, since these are cheap and malt is relatively dear.

Draining of wort, sparging: The mash tun is a large metal vessel with a false bottom, with provision for stirring the wort steadily. After two or three hours at the right temperature, the wort is drained away. Since quite a lot can still be recovered from the residue, warm water is sprayed through it. By this process, called sparging, the last of the wort is extracted.

Boiling with hops: The wort is boiled with dried hops for about two hours. Hops contain tannin, which later helps to clear the beer; oils which provide the essential flavour of beer; resins which act as a preservative and provide bitter flavour; and more diastase. The trouble is that a great deal of the valuable content of hops is lost in boiling. It is common therefore to add fresh hops near the end of the boiling, or later when the beer is very nearly ready.

Cooling: While heat is obviously an essential part of the production of beer, it carries its dangers at various stages in the process. Too much heat can kill the malt early on, and overhot mashing defeats its own purpose. There is, too, the risk of the formation of acetic acid, which increases above 65° C. The wort is therefore cooled as quickly as possible to about 15° C.

Yeasting and fermentation: The wort is run into fermenting tanks and yeast is added. This is usually top-working yeast, but the recent increase in popularity of lagers, which are produced by a bottom-working yeast, has resulted in wider use of bottom yeasts not only for lagers but also for similar pale beers. Plenty of yeast is used, because although theoretically an ounce of yeast would eventually grow sufficiently to be capable of fermenting a thousand gallons, this would take a long time, with the danger of spoilage always present. A thick head forms on the surface. Activity during fermentation can be tumultuous. After a day or two or a week, depending on the amount of sugar to be fermented, the top yeast is skimmed off. The beer is again drained off. It is beer now, not wort any longer.

Settling, priming and fining: So far the story of all beers is similar, except in the drying or roasting of the malt before

27

mashing. From now on the beer can be handled in many different ways. There is a lot of yeast left and it has to be removed somehow. There may be further skimming. Dry hops added at this stage not only restore lost flavour, but also in settling carry down with them any yeast which remains. Isinglass fining may be used.

Priming, or sweetening, also occurs now, if necessary. Beers such as sweet stout are sweetened by lactose, not sugar, because sugar would start further fermentation and lactose doesn't.

Racking: The beer is racked, and depending on its type may be bottled, sent out in cask or stored for weeks or months. Bottled beers are carbonated like any ordinary fizzy drink.

This is only an outline of what is obviously a very complicated process, but it contains most of what the amateur beer maker should know about how commercial beer is produced.

Anyone who wants to make beer himself must follow in broad outline the method described above—there's no other way. Corners can be cut by using prepared materials, but that merely means that somebody else has done part of the job.

Here are some of the differences between commercial and home brewing:

Making malt at home is not really practicable. There is no harm in trying some experiments. But unless you have facilities not found in the average house, germination of barley will either be a flop or will entail more labour than it's worth. So bought malt must be used.

It's easy enough to crush malt with a rolling-pin, in a coffee

28

grinder or with a suitable food-mixer attachment. That's no problem. Anyway, crushing is not essential.

Mashing simply can't be done as the brewers do it unless you buy or make a mash tun. Large vessels with false bottoms are unwieldy anyway. The simplest substitute method is to heat the malt to the correct temperature in an ordinary cooking pot. It's desirable but not essential, after mashing is complete, to boil the whole of the wort with hops. An extract of a gallon or two can be made up to the right quantity with cold water.

The home brewer doesn't have to worry about cooling. He's dealing with small quantities and watching over them. There should be no risk of contamination or acetification.

Yeasting and fermentation in a plastic bucket can produce perfectly good results. In this stage of the proceedings the brewers hold no advantages.

In the final stages the home beer maker diverges completely from commercial practice. He can't, in particular, carbonate his beer—he has to let residual yeast do it for him.

What must be remembered is that the commercial method and the home method both work. If a commercial method is impracticable for the home brewer, he must find a substitute. Fortunately, perfectly adequate substitute methods are available at all stages.

Home brew can be very good indeed. It can even be superb. The professionals don't always have to win.

CHAPTER III

What goes in

Double, double toil and trouble;
Fire burn, and cauldron bubble.
Round about the cauldron go;
In the malted barley throw.
Hops well dried in oven hot
Simmer well i' the charmèd pot.
Add for strength that it will yield
Sugar from a tropic field.
And now about the cauldron sing,
Like elves and fairies in a ring,
Enchanting all that you put in.

SHAKESPEARE, *Macbeer*

So you're going to make some beer. What do you have to have? And what do you have to understand?

The second, oddly enough, is far more important than the first. When one hears of atrocities in ale making, of disasters too dire to describe, it always turns out on investigation that the criminal didn't really know the gun was loaded. Or he didn't know which way to point it.

If you have the faintest general idea of how to go about making beer, you can never produce any brew that's undrinkable.

30

WHAT GOES IN

The first important factor is the exact nature of the water supply. Water in your area may be hard or soft or anything in between. It is likely to have certain trace elements peculiar to the locality. Although various water treatments are available, and they are effective in their way, only by distilling the water and then putting back in it what we want for our particular purpose could we make the water in our own district identical to the water readily available in another region. This, of course, is quite impracticable.

It is therefore sensible to make the kind of beer for which the water supply in your district is particularly suited. In general, pale ales and bitter beers are best in a hard-water district, and stout in a soft-water region.

However, if you want to make a whole range of different beers and do the job properly from scratch, scratch in this case being water, the things you need are calcium sulphate and sodium carbonate.

Burton ales are made from water with a rather high percentage of calcium sulphate (gypsum). This is quite cheap and readily obtainable. If your water is soft and you want to make pale ale or bitter beer, add half a teaspoonful of gypsum to each gallon.

Water for stout should be soft. It should have a minimum of dissolved salts, or only salts which will be precipitated in boiling, such as magnesium acid carbonates. If your water is hard and you want to make stout or mild ale, boil the water with sodium carbonate. This will precipitate the calcium and magnesium sulphates.

Malt can be bought in many forms. As grain you can buy pale malt, crystal malt, black malt or patent black malt. It is obtainable, light or dark, in powder form. And the easiest way to get it, if there isn't a beer equipment supplier in the area, is in the form of liquid malt extract, obtainable from any chemist.

Take care if you buy malt extract from a chemist that you get plain, ordinary malt extract. The extract with cod- or halibut-liver oil is quite useless, and should not be tried even experimentally. Also there are certain other preparations which the chemist may assure you are just as good as malt extract, or better. Better they may be for an invalid, taken by the dessertspoon, but if they contain extra ingredients they may well be as useless for beer making as extract with cod-liver oil.

For the home brewer, malt in the form of an extract, powder or liquid, is much easier to use than grain malt, and liquid malt extract is by far the most economical form. Although some extracts bought from chemists can cost as much as 4s. a pound, these are really intended for health purposes and entirely suitable malt extract can be obtained, in quantity, at just over 1s. a pound.

It is hard to say whether there is any difference in quality solely due to the use of grain rather than extract, or vice versa. Many people swear there is, of course—there are always traditionalists who insist that all old ways must be right just because they are old. Personally I am quite unable to tell by testing beer whether the basic ingredient was malt grain or extract.

It is true that a wider variety of malt is obtainable as grain —at least four types, more if you count the variations between different crystal malts, for example—and that extract, liquid or dried, is generally obtainable only light or dark. For this reason mixtures are often used. If you want to make a moderately dark beer, ordinary malt extract can be used as the basis, with a little black malt or patent black malt to supply colour and taste.

Certainly if some grain malt is used with malt extract it becomes virtually impossible to detect by the taste that malt extract rather than grain malt only is the basis of the brew.

Hops are now just as essential as malt in brewing, although it was not always so. No beer, ale, lager or stout is made without hops.

Hops are obtainable dried or as hop extract.

If it's hard to tell the difference in the finished beer made with malt and with extract, there's no difficulty at all in distinguishing between beer flavoured with hops and with hop extract. Dried hops win hands down.

This is a great pity, for several reasons. To begin with, hop extract is relatively cheaper than hops. Then, as the methods of commercial brewers clearly indicate, dry hops demand expert knowledge and great care if the best use is to be made of them. Finally, and shatteringly, hops stink.

If we're not going to call a spade an agricultural implement, there's no getting round the fact that hops make well-rotted manure smell like eau-de-Cologne. In their dried form they make their presence felt in a room. An ordinary paper bag doesn't contain them; the odour escapes like Houdini. A plastic bag beats them, though. When they're boiled in water, the smell is different but not more attractive. And it's one of those smells, like those of damp raincoats and boiled fish, which linger about a house interminably.

(Personal note: for a long time I was forced to use hop extract, which doesn't smell, or not make beer at all. I didn't mind the smell too much, but I was strenuously outvoted. Then it came about that on one day a week I had the house to myself for about twelve hours, and boiled hops on that day. The smell isn't gone at the end of twelve hours, but it is tolerable.)

There it is. As in the case of malt, hop extract used with hops becomes a much better proposition. Some of the cost can be saved and the beer is first-class. But if you're going to boil an ounce of hops (which is a surprisingly large bulk since dried hops are very light), you may as well boil half a pound or so. The smell doesn't seem to be much worse.

For an 'easy' beer, hop extract, or the hop-flavoured malt extract already mentioned, can be confidently recommended. It's certainly a much less arduous process when the hop-boiling stage is omitted. And if you've never made beer before, you'll probably be delighted with the result and feel other methods are quite unnecessary, since a beer so good can be made so easily.

But as time passes the desire to make a still better beer becomes stronger. A better beer can be made with malt and hop extract, some extra grain, additions such as water treatment, citric acid, tannin, salt, oil and hops, heading liquid and more attention to detail. For real quality, however, you must use dried hops and some grain malt.

With water, malt and hops you can make beer, perhaps the best beer. There is no need to use sugar or extra grain. These are used not for added quality but for cheapness.

I understand that in South Germany the use of sugar in beer is still banned. Well, if you've drunk Löwenbräu or Paulanerbräu in Munich, you can see the point. These are the best beers in the world (except some of your own, of course).

And for the home beer maker who is more concerned about quality than cost, hops, malt and water will suffice.

Most of us, however, would choose to make five gallons of excellent beer rather than two gallons of even bettter beer at the same price. So sugar and grain are the next two items to be considered.

It has been stated that malt at mashing temperature, 65° C, produces more diastase than is necessary to convert the starch present in the malt itself. Now malt costs about one and sixpence a pound. Broken maize costs about sixpence. It therefore makes sense to include in the mash some cheap grain to provide extra starch and body.

Almost anything will do—maize, barley, wheat, oats, rye, potatoes, rice, tapioca and no doubt quite a few more things, not all of them grain.

Choice is dictated not so much by the result, which is similar in all cases, but by cost and ease of handling.

No beer making processes have been described in detail so far, except the instant wort method and the commercial technique. But straining will almost certainly be necessary, and it is advisable to use as extra grain something which strains easily.

Oatmeal makes a thick gruel or porage, not surprisingly, since this is what porage is made with. This doesn't strain at all well or easily. Rice in any form swells and clumps.

The easiest grain to handle is broken maize, with barley a close second. And broken maize is very cheap.

Sugar is used mainly to save money It's not just that sugar

costs only about half as much as malt, though it does. When you consider that the spent malt grains, when finally thrown away, must weigh quite a bit, and that not all the extract from the grains is maltose, it's clear that weight for weight there's far more sugar in sugar than in malt.

Ordinary white sugar is perfectly adequate. Demerara or other brown sugar can be used, and they impart qualities of their own, but more is needed than of ordinary sugar.

Invert sugar is best, because in effect this is partly fermented already. The yeast doesn't have to split the sugar into glucose and fructose, because this is already done.

Invert sugar is dearer than ordinary household sugar, and more of it is necessary, which makes it dearer still. Therefore if you want to use invert sugar, the use of which isn't essential except perhaps in winter, the best thing to do is make it yourself. All you do is boil it gently with a little citric acid, using the syrup so formed instead of dry sugar.

It should be remembered that sugar as we know it is a very recent discovery. Beer, or at any rate ale, was made thousands of years before anything resembling household sugar existed.

Honey has always been around, and until fairly recently honey was the *only* common sweetening agent. Since honey contains a great deal of vegetable matter, it is perfectly capable of sustaining a fermentation on its own. The alcohol so formed was the famous mead which was the drink of the heroes, and others who weren't heroic at all.

Honey can still be used in beer, but the cost is prohibitive, unless you buy Australian or Canadian honey in bulk. It would be best to add honey to the wort before boiling, since it may contain bacteria that would ruin the fermentation.

But honey, syrup, treacle and other sweeteners should be

used only experimentally. It must be stressed again that the best beer is probably made from the right water, malt and hops, and nothing else. It may be, of course, that individual taste will cause the rejection of so-called best beer in favour of honey- or treacle-flavoured beer, or one of the thousand other variations available. Nevertheless, a standard beer should be tried first. Then, if you wish, try bizarre ingredients.

Syrup, which had better be called golden syrup to distinguish it from the sugar dissolved in water we generally call syrup in beer and wine making, can be used as a substitute for sugar. Only a liking for the peculiar taste it imparts could commend it.

Treacle, on the other hand, is a useful addition on account of both taste and colour. Although again it provides a flavour which won't be to everybody's taste, so does caramel, the other ingredient commonly used to darken beer.

You can't really darken beer without changing the taste. Admittedly I haven't tried any of the food dyes intended merely to change the colour without changing the taste. Such a dye is used in the production of kippers. People expect kippers to be golden to dark brown, and a dye is used to provide the colour. Experiments tried at fish research centres have established, not really surprisingly, that people don't like green or blue or purple kippers, even if the taste is exactly the same as that of brown kippers.

The natural way to change the colour of beer is to use more or a different variety of malt. This changes the taste anyway. Beer made from black malt tastes quite different from beer made with crystal malt.

Caramel is often recommended. Caramel is caramelized or burnt sugar, analogous to roasted malt. You can buy it as gravy browning, but be careful you get plain browning, described on the label as caramel. Gravy powder or gravy salt contains ingredients such as salt, monosodium glutamate, hydrolysed protein, beef extract, parsley, spices and flavouring which may or may not spoil the beer for you. Use of such materials should be regarded as experimental.

Caramel also affects the taste, although only at most a couple of teaspoons are included in four or five gallons. Since taste is so personal a matter that the word has a wide abstract use, the only recommendation that can safely be made is this:

First make a beer quite regardless of colour. It may turn out paler than any beer you ever saw. It won't be very dark unless you started off with patent black malt, which isn't a very good idea. The paleness of a beer just faintly yellowish needn't prevent it from being a very good light ale of the lager type. However, if you want to darken it, use some darker malt—*some*, not the entire quantity used. This will teach your palate the difference inherent in various malts. Later, if you wish, try caramel, but don't exceed one teaspoon in five gallons at first. Then try treacle, not more than a pound in five gallons, dissolved in the hot wort.

In this way you will avoid the tragedy of brewing say five gallons of perfectly sound beer that you don't happen to like. There are few greater dilemmas—do you flagellate yourself by forcing yourself to drink it, or perhaps more so by pouring it down the drain?

Yeast is the most important ingredient of all, and never more so when you don't use any. This isn't an Irishism. Leave anything which is capable of fermentation alone for a while, and almost invariably it will ferment if left long

enough. This is due partly to the wild yeasts which exist every-
where, and partly to the fact that it's very difficult to kill
yeast and make sure it stays dead. So if you don't add
a selected yeast, the fermentation will be controlled by some
wild yeast you haven't selected, probably the wrong one.

Yeast will be considered more fully in a chapter on yeast
alone. Meantime, the recommendation already given can't be
improved upon: obtain a genuine bottom-working beer
yeast and use that.

CHAPTER IV

What used to go in

What two ideas are more inseparable than Beer and Britannia?
REV. SYDNEY SMITH

In the beginning, there was beer. No, that's not profane. There were many other things too, but they're outside the scope of this book.

It seems that all primitive societies, the moment they find themselves becoming societies, start brewing. Whenever a nomad tribe settles down anywhere, grain is grown, and the moment grain is grown, some kind of beer is made from it.

Anything which will make bread will make beer. It's no coincidence that grain and yeast are used in making bread. Grain and yeast are all that is needed to make beer—or, more accurately historically, ale.

The origin of ale is lost in antiquity, as is the origin of bread. The Egyptians, the Greeks and the Romans certainly knew all about it, but that's practically modern history. All the indications are that umpteen thousand years ago beer of some kind was brewed. The ancient Britons undoubtedly made it without having to be shown how by the Romans.

But this was *ale*, which, correctly, is a malt liquor without the addition of hops. The Romans are said to have introduced the hop to Britain, although this should be taken, as they might have said themselves, *cum grano salis*. If this was so, it seems strange that 1,500 years should elapse before hops came into general use, and two or three centuries more before ale (unhopped beer) disappeared.

Ale (without hops) was imbibed for centuries on end. It can be tasted now by any home brewer—he merely has to leave hops out of a bottle or two. It is a bland, too bland drink, sweetish, tasteless, obviously needing something. Tasting it, you might reach for the Worcester sauce or curry power. It can be as strong as the strongest beer, but the flavour is insipid.

Every home brewer should at one time or another taste this original ale for himself. It should be racked, primed and matured exactly like beer; the only difference is that no flavouring is added. The experience will not be supremely rapturous. Its value is to show the role hops play and give some indication of the strength of hop flavouring various beers require.

It is easy, after this test, to understand how the taste of hops, in the very first bitters, insinuated itself into the rugged British palate.

Before hops, other flavours were used—nettles, rosemary, burdock, ivy. One thing was obvious—*some* flavour was needed.

Even now it is very well worth while to do some cautious experimentation with flavours other than hops. You may find something you like better than hopped beer.

The basis should always be the same. Of course, hops add more than just flavour to beer, and some of the herbs used for herb beer do not. Anyway, wort is made with malt in the ordinary way, sugared in the ordinary way, and fermented. The only difference is that instead of hops, or in addition to hops, other flavourings are used.

Many of the suppliers of ginger, cut root of burdock, dandelion, sarsaparilla and spruce for herb beers, sometimes called botanical herbs, supply instructions calling for the use of water, yeast, sugar and flavouring only. Although these may produce quite pleasant drinks, it's only fair to give the experiment a chance by giving the flavour proper support, that is, a malt liquor base. After all, you're not comparing maltless sarsaparilla with maltless hop beer.

Top of the list is spruce. And the taste may not be entirely unfamiliar, because spruce is used in Scandinavian beers. Like hops, spruce acts as a preservative.

The only snag is that the form of spruce oil usually supplied is so concentrated that it's hard to control the quantity. After all, when a half ounce of oil will flavour eight gallons of beer there's a risk, when smaller quantities are made, of getting far too much flavour in one batch and not nearly enough in another. The simplest way of dealing with this is to mix the concentrate with a larger quantity of water which can easily be measured.

Spruce makes a good partner for hops.

It is unfortunately impossible to give very much guidance about the use of these various flavourings. How does one describe a taste?

For instance, sarsaparilla beer has a very strong taste (and smell), but all one can tell someone who has never tasted sarsaparilla beer is that it's black, rather like liquorice, rather like treacle, not unlike beer made with patent black malt. So now you know whether you'll like sarsaparilla beer or not?

The taste of ginger so-called beer is well known. In this context, however, we're dealing with something very different from the non-alcoholic, artificially aerated drink now sold as ginger beer.

Real ginger beer can be made in scores of different ways. The stone ginger of a century and more ago was yeasted and therefore must have been at least mildly alcoholic. A pleasant and potent drink can be made by flavouring malt ale with ground ginger. If malt is not included, root ginger should be used, well crushed, with citric and tartaric acid and sugar in a mild fermentation. Yeast nutrient will be needed because there is nothing much else in such a brew to support a steady fermentation.

Ginger essence is obtainable from beer equipment suppliers, and instructions are included.

People who like to experiment for experiment's sake, or who sincerely wish to train their palates by tasting different ingredients as nearly as possible isolated, should try hop beer, that is, beer made without malt. Frankly, it isn't very good. Malt has been advised as the basis for all these experiments in flavouring, because thus there will be a sound unflavoured ale base, of any desired strength, and the flavouring has the same opportunity as hops to show what it can do. Yet if you're going to try out the thin brews which result from fermentations of essence, sugar, water, yeast nutrient, your experiments will be incomplete unless you compare hops, on this basis, with spruce, sarsaparilla, ginger, burdock, dandelion, etc. You need about an ounce of hops per gallon, half a pound of sugar per gallon, yeast and yeast nutrient. The hops are boiled as in the normal extraction process, some fresh hops being added near the end of the boiling.

This is not suggested as a remarkably fine beer. It should be tried only if you really want to know how hops perform in the absence of malt, and particularly if you make other unhopped and unmalted beers.

The easiest and least potentially disastrous way to experiment with the various flavours other than hops is to get hold of the necessary oil, extract or root in the smallest quantity available and use it to flavour a few bottles of ale made without hops. The rest can be flavoured with hop extract after racking.

But it must never be forgotten that in commercial practice the hop has established itself as a hands-down winner. If other herbs were as much to popular taste, it would be possible to walk into any bar and ask for dandelion beer or sarsaparilla beer or burdock beer. Experiment at your own risk . . . I might have used as a quotation at the head of this chapter, with special reference to hopped beer, G. K. Chesterton's lines:

> *If an angel out of heaven*
> *Brings you other things to drink,*
> *Thank him for his kind attentions,*
> *Go and pour them down the sink.*

CHAPTER V

Don't overdo it

Not drunk is he who from the floor
Can rise alone and still drink more;
But drunk is he, who prostrate lies,
Without the power to drink or rise.

T. L. PEACOCK

Now let's consider one important point very soberly, while we still can.

How strong do you want to make your beer?

This is a serious matter, and the sad thing is that only experience, and usually unfortunate experience at that, ever seems to get the point across.

It is possible to make beer of virtually any strength. I can't tell you the top limits, and I don't know anyone who can, because beer makers with enough experience to achieve these limits don't try.

Whisky can make a man very drunk very quickly. But whisky, among civilized drinkers, is taken in very small quantities, often with water, and usually slowly.

Sherry and port are intermediate drinks, not nearly as strong as whisky, brandy, rum, gin and vodka, but stronger than ordinary wines. This is because both have brandy added to them.

Genuine sweet wines such as Sauternes, Tokay and Johannisberg *trockenbeerenauslese* are no weaklings either. You drink them by the glass, slowly.

Dry wines are less potent. Moselles and the light hocks, particularly, can be drunk fairly freely with very little risk of a hangover next morning.

But all these are drunk in relatively small quantities, and not rapidly. The true wine drinker, and he isn't necessarily a snob, smells first, then sips. The hog who knocks back a glass of good wine and instantly holds out his glass for more should be sent to the torture chambers. Certainly he shouldn't get another glass until he's learned how to drink it.

Beer in all countries, even countries like Germany which make good wine and good beer, is a different kind of drink. People drink it when they are thirsty, when they are in company, or just to pass the time. One drink has no effect on anybody, unless he isn't used to it. Anyway, if time isn't pressing, he naturally intends to have considerably more than one drink.

Beer is a drink to hold in your hand, to laugh with, to sing community songs with.

The trouble is that if you make your own, you can make it as strong as wine—probably stronger, with a little ingenuity, for malt ferments better than almost anything, at least as well as grapes.

So you can land up with a pint in your hand which can easily finish you off, not permanently, but certainly for the evening—at 8 p.m. Who wants that?

The beer drinker expects to rise from the floor and drink

more. He never expects to lie prostrate, without the power to drink or rise.

More than that—he doesn't expect to land on the floor in the first place.

Don't make your beer too strong—but do make a lot of beer.

It must be admitted that once you start making beer so easily and cheaply that a man who can afford to pay off the mortgage on a house can afford to drink beer all day and every day, your consumption is liable to go up. That's part of the reason for the warning about strength.

When supplies, time and a man's purse are limited, there are many factors working to prevent him drinking too much. By the time he's had a little too much, it's 'Time, gentlemen, please.' Although he may keep beer in the house, the fact that a can costs about two shillings and sixpence can be forgotten only occasionally, not all day and every day. Besides, if he and his wife and a few friends get to work on even a healthy stock, one evening can make it sick and two can kill it. But when it takes only half an hour's work and a few shillings' worth of materials to ensure a good supply (admittedly at least two weeks ahead), such considerations no longer apply.

Also, soon after a man (or woman) starts making beer, experimentally in the first place, one of two things happens. Either for one reason or another he gives up making beer, or he starts doing it regularly, systematically, so that just as the last batch is finished the next is matured enough to be drunk. This means that there's always some kind of beer in the house. Therefore if the current brew is killed prematurely, owing perhaps to unexpected visitors, it's always possible to drink the next brew too soon. It won't be at its best—but thirsty people are notoriously uncritical.

This reinforces what has been said already. If, temperamentally, you are the kind of person who can't stop, it is unwise for you to start something that may get out of hand.

The vast majority of wine and beer makers in this country are people who can not only hold but can also keep their liquor. They have to be. There are many cellars in the country which could sustain their owners in constant inebriation for months or even years. Yet they don't succumb any more than anybody else. Why?

Well, it's the difference between an individual or household that can keep three-quarters of a bottle of whisky in a cocktail cabinet for weeks on end without thinking about it, and the individual or household that can't have a bottle on hand without killing it.

Beer is peculiarly a drink which people want to go on drinking. It's significant that in the average pub most people stay until closing time. Some people come in for a couple of drinks and go away again. Some leave a few minutes early. But every pub doing good business is jammed to the gunnels just before the bell rings.

Therefore, at the risk of repetition—make a lot of weak beer. Don't make strong beer except for special occasions, when you quite frankly intend to drink too much. If such occasions don't exist in your life, don't make strong beer at all.

The advice given to peppery old gentlemen with red noses —'Put more water in it'—is good advice to beer makers. A method designed for two gallons of excellent, very strong beer can produce, simply by the addition of water, five gallons of pleasant, virtually harmless beer. There is a kind of natural law—more malt, more hops; more strength, more bitterness. Thus a properly balanced strong brew is turned into a more or less well balanced weak brew by the addition of water and nothing else.

But this, it must be clearly understood, is before fermentation. You can't pour a third of a glass of strong beer, finished beer, top it up with water and get a decent drink. (You can, as a shandy, top up with gassy lemonade, which like beer contains carbon dioxide.) You have to add the extra water before the fermentation starts.

Quantities of malt, hops and sugar to use are discussed in the next chapter. Meantime, a rough working rule is this. If the weight of malt plus sugar exceeds one pound per gallon, you're entering the region of medium to strong beer. At a combined weight of one pound per gallon you're still in the comparatively safe region of mild beers.

No alcoholic drink is ever a hundred per cent safe—it would be a contradiction in terms if it were. There have been cases of children becoming mildly tipsy now that shandies including a little beer can be easily obtained. Ordinary cider has crept up on people who had no intention of becoming affected at all, and the more potent ciders are notorious for their deceptive strength. They taste almost like appleade, and they have a kick like a mule.

Nevertheless, beer can be made so mild that although it is very satisfying, especially in hot weather, with a fine tang and prickle and first-class thirst-quenching properties, it can't noticeably affect an experienced beer drinker. I'm assuming that genuine beer drinkers would no more dream of knocking

back a pint at a gulp and getting a refill at once than a genuine
wine drinker would drink good wine like a thirsty dog drinking water. It does, and it should, take time to drink a pint.
Good beer should be sipped and tasted, not thrown back
down the gullet with hardly any contact with the taste-buds
at all.

Fifteen minutes? Half an hour? An hour? There isn't likely
to be general agreement on the time it takes to get full satisfaction from a pint of beer. But it certainly isn't one minute or
five.

And if drinking time for a pint of mild *averages* an hour
—that's counting eating, going to the bathroom, putting out
the dog, answering the telephone and pouring the next pint—
your beer can really be harmless.

But you have to make it so. . . .

Arbitrarily, it has been assumed virtually throughout that
five gallons of beer will be made at a time. There is nothing
magical about five gallons. A convenient quantity for a
particular brewer could be three or four or six or eight.

Home-brewed beer doesn't keep indefinitely, especially
weak beer. For various other reasons, beer is generally made
in weekly or fortnightly batches. The job of bottling a whole
month's supply tends to be a tedious chore. Besides, you need
a forest of bottles.

The arbitrary assumption is likely to be found the most
convenient: make up about two gallons of wort for a strong
ale; fill it up to five gallons for a weak beer; ferment, bottle,
mature, drink, and repeat *ad infinitum*, or until you sign the
pledge.

Your friends will be sorry when you do.

CHAPTER VI

Look before you leap

A little learning is a dangerous thing;
Drink deep, or taste not the Pierian spring:
There shallow draughts intoxicate the brain,
And drinking largely sobers us again.

ALEXANDER POPE

All recipes should be used with caution and, if possible, intelligence. Published recipes, compared, occasionally cause beginners to scratch their heads, if not tear their hair out by the roots in frustration. Some recommend two ounces of hops, a pound of sugar and two pounds of malt per gallon; others less than half an ounce of hops, half a pound of malt and half a pound of sugar. The beginner wonders, not unreasonably, if the larger quantities are really necessary. If so, the more modest recipe must produce a ghost of a beer. On the other hand, if good beer can be made from the second recipe, why squander ingredients as in the first?

The first recipe is for a very strong beer and the second for a light ale—but that's only half the story.

As Lewis Carroll might have said, the more you eat the more you can eat. The more you drink the more you can drink. The more ingredients you put in a recipe, the more you

51

have to put in. There is a certain jabberwocky truth in all these statements.

A strong beer with a very bland flavour is not only a cheat and a liar, it's an offence against nature. At least, natural palates find it so. When we detect considerable body in beer, we expect a lot of tang, a great deal of bitterness, to go with it. Otherwise the beer is a baffling, perverse hybrid. It tastes almost like a light ale and it blows your head off—a most unfriendly act.

It is impossible not to have sympathy with the unfortunate friends of an enthusiastic but misguided tyro beer maker. He has not yet come to appreciate any of the points made in the last chapter. His beer is of hair-raising potency, and he's proud of it. But hops are expensive, compared with sugar, in the relevant proportions. So he hops for a mild beer and sugars with demoniac enthusiasm. The result, usually, is a syrupy, rather tasteless brew, and friends used only to commercial beers are almost certain to dismiss it as a harmless concoction, not actively unpleasant, and drink a pint or two, or three. . . .

I'd be sorry for anyone—among the friends, that is—who got into trouble in such circumstances. After all, how could *he* know the gun was loaded?

So when a beer is strong, it should also be bitter. Bitterness doesn't necessarily imply unpleasantness. The experiment already suggested of testing genuine ale (unhopped) for taste is very valuable in the beer maker's repertoire of experience. He will find it rather like eating fish and chips with sugar instead of salt and vinegar. A few sips will show him why the astringency of hops is vital in beer.

Strong beers, therefore, must be well hopped. Light ales should not be, as a rule.

LOOK BEFORE YOU LEAP

In commercial beer, hop flavour, if anything, is often stronger than the alcoholic content of the beer demands. Consequently the beer appears to be stronger than it is. The reason is probably the excise system of basing duty on the specific gravity of the wort.   .

Unlike the amateur wine maker, the beer maker doesn't really have to know anything about specific gravity and the use of the hydrometer at all. He can follow rules of thumb like the following:

Table for five gallons

	HARMLESS ALE	MILD ALE	MEDIUM BEER	STRONG ALE	VIOLENT ALE
Malt	1½ lb.	2 lb.	2 lb.	4 lb.	6 lb.
Hops	2 oz.	4 oz.	6 oz.	6 oz.	8 oz.
Sugar	2 lb.	3 lb.	4 lb.	3 lb.	4 lb.
Maize	—	½ lb.	1 lb.	1 lb.	1 lb.

There is nothing mystical about these figures, and they don't have to be remembered or even referred to if you remember the principles:

Less than 1 lb. total malt and sugar per gallon: very weak beer.

More than 1 lb. total malt and sugar per gallon: a normal ale.

As much as 2 lb. total malt and sugar per gallon: strong beer.

For weak beers, about ½ oz. of hops per gallon.

For medium beers, about 1 oz. of hops per gallon.

For strong beers, up to 2 oz. of hops per gallon.

The rule is very simple—take 1 lb. (for malt and sugar)

and 1 oz. (hops) as the dividing line. Below: weak. Above: strong.

Although it isn't a rule, it is a good practice to keep the quantities of malt and sugar roughly similar, bearing in mind that the best beers of all are probably those in which so much malt is used that it's unnecessary to use sugar at all. At any rate, don't let the quantities of sugar go galloping ahead of the quantities of malt. Five gallons of beer made with 1½ lb. of malt and 5 lb. of sugar would probably ferment quite well with a good yeast, and the beer would be fairly strong. However, whether 2 oz. or 6 oz. of hops were also used, the beer would be pale and spectral, and would have the distinctive taste of an undermalted ale, a taste not present in an innocuous beer made with 1½ lb. of malt and only 2 lb. of sugar. Malt doesn't supply a lot of the taste in beer, but it supplies practically all the body, which is something quite independent of the actual alcoholic strength.

This explains the one small apparent inconsistency in the table. In every case except one, as the ale gets stronger more malt, sugar and hops are required. But in strong ale, compared with an average beer, twice as much malt is given with less sugar. This is because strong ale as we understand it doesn't have to be particularly potent, but it has to taste as if it were. Strong ale made on this basis will be only moderately potent and not excessively bitter, but it will have enough body to satisfy anybody except the hard drinker.

Even the beer described as violent ale is not nearly as strong as we could make it, nor has it the bitterness which a really strong ale would demand. It is submitted, however, as the strongest brew that any ordinary beer drinker should make. Anything above this and you're liable to enter the unsavoury

LOOK BEFORE YOU LEAP

area of drinking to get drunk, of guests passing out, of hang-overs the next day.

Of course, if you propose to drink beer as a kind of liqueur, in small glasses and with due ritual, the strongest beer it's possible to make would not be out of place. But such practices are for the specialist, not the ordinary beer drinker.

Although you don't have to use a hydrometer, its use is desirable. Then you can calculate the strength of any beer you make. More important than the figures themselves is the fact that you can in this way compare your beers and know just how strong any particular beer is going to be. You can also standardize your favourite beers, so that when you hit on one you like better than most you can produce it again at will. And, perhaps even more important, you can pick the right moment to bottle, not so late that the beer cannot produce gas and remains flat, not so early that when opened the bottle erupts foam like a fire-extinguisher and you're left with about an inch of yeasty froth at the bottom of the bottle.

Hydrometers are used for many purposes, one of them being to check the specific gravity of acid in a battery. You therefore have to get the right kind of hydrometer for beer making, and since you'll have to find a supplier of malt, hops, etc., probably a specialist in wine-making sundries, it would be sensible to obtain a hydrometer from him. Then you can be sure you don't get one for measuring the acid in batteries.

When it arrives you'll find it's a weighted glass bulb with a long calibrated tail, so designed that it floats upright in water. You can if you like buy a test jar with it, but this isn't vital— a milk bottle or cordial bottle with a fairly wide neck will do.

Floated in plain water, the hydrometer sinks almost its

full length to read 1·000. A simple experiment will show exactly what the instrument is for. Dissolve a little sugar in the water, and the hydrometer will rise. It now reads 1·010 or 1·015. As more sugar is added, the hydrometer rises until the whole tail is out of the water.

The application of the hydrometer is obvious. It measures the sugar content and therefore the alcohol potential.

Naturally the hydrometer can't distinguish between sugar and other solvents which affect the specific gravity (the reading obtained). Salt would do the same kind of thing. In the kind of liquid prepared for fermentation, however, the reading can be taken as sugar content, including sugar from malt and other grain, or from syrup or treacle.

Suppose your cooled wort, made up to the final volume and ready for fermentation, gives a reading of 1·040. Once fermentation starts, the yeast will vigorously convert sugar into alcohol, the specific gravity of which is lower than that of water (below 1·000), and carbon dioxide, which escapes. So the reading drops. Eventually it could drop to 1·000, which doesn't mean that your beer has become water again, but that virtually all the sugar present in the beginning has been fermented to alcohol and gas. It is then safe to bottle.

For convenience, we note readings in a simpler form. A specific gravity between 1·070 and 1·080 can produce a hair-raisingly potent beer (10% alcohol, considerably greater than the alcohol content of a light white wine, which may be as little as 7%). Beer seldom has enough alcohol in it for the reading to drop below 1·000, as often happens with wine. We are therefore concerned only with the range between 1·000 and 1·080, so it's convenient to use merely the last two figures —0, 10, 25, 45, 80.

LOOK BEFORE YOU LEAP

Since we are not going to encounter readings below zero or above 80, the type of hydrometer to buy is one with a range 1·000 to 1·100. You could buy one reading 1·000 to 1·200 or 1·300, but since the smaller the range the greater the accuracy, the 1·000–1·100 hydrometer really has no competition.

The hydrometer has many uses. First, in mashing and boiling the same or similar ingredients don't always produce the same result. An S.G. expected to be 43 may turn out to be only 34. The method and materials may have been identical, but for some reason the extraction process was not as efficient. Perhaps mashing temperature was too high or too low, or mashing didn't go on long enough. Anyway, whatever happened, you can put it right by adding sugar until the reading reaches 43.

The point is, there would be no way of knowing anything was wrong if you didn't have a hydrometer. The finished beer would turn out weaker than you expected, and next time, to get it right, you'd increase the malt and sugar. If the mashing happened to be more efficient this time, this might well result in an initial S.G. of 55, giving you a very strong ale, stronger than you normally get in a pub, with perhaps unfortunate results.

A hydrometer check at this point, just before the fermentation starts, is well worth while, because every now and then the reading is unexpected. If you have forgotten to put in the sugar (and this can happen), the reading will tell you what has happened before any harm is done. If you've been making a different quantity from your usual, a muddle may have occurred and you get a reading right off the scale, that is, greater than 100. Such a brew might not ferment at all. Anyway, the obvious thing to do would be to dilute it considerably.

Readings must be taken when the liquid is cool but not cold. They are accurate only at 60° F. (the hydrometer has this figure printed on it). Since this is a comfortable room temperature there's no problem at all. The point should be borne in mind, however, in very cold or very hot weather. If you want an accurate reading, not just a general indication, make sure the wort *is* at 60° F. Either wait until late at night when the temperature has dropped, or heat the room to the correct temperature.

Hydrometer readings during the progress of fermentation are not necessary, although many beer makers keep a routine record of every brew for their own satisfaction. Certainly if anything seems to be wrong, the first thing to do is take a reading.

Suppose you're uncertain of the condition of the yeast. One fermentation may give a set of readings like this:

Initial gravity	35
1st day	15
2nd day	5
3rd day	0

Another, with identical wort, goes (or rather doesn't go) like this:

Initial gravity	35
1st day	35
2nd day	35
3rd day	35
4th day	35

Well, your yeast is dead. You put it in when the wort was too hot. Or you forgot to put it in at all. Or it had somehow been accidentally roasted. So you yeast the wort again.

LOOK BEFORE YOU LEAP

When an inactive, though correct, yeast is added direct to the wort, this kind of reading may occur:

Initial gravity	35
1st day	35
2nd day	35
3rd day	35
4th day	31
5th day	22
6th day	15
7th day	10
8th day	7
9th day	5
10th day	3

When you consider that a beer maker who never uses a hydrometer might bottle every one of these brews after a week (an average figure), the hydrometer no longer appears to be a luxury item at all. Every one of these beers would be spoiled. The first would be too inactive to create gas in the bottle. The second never fermented at all. The third would probably burst all the bottles once the yeast, only coming back to peak condition, as the progress of the fermentation shows, finally attained its full vigour, with quite a lot of sugar left to work on.

The hydrometer can also be used to establish the percentage of alcohol by volume in your beer. You need the initial S.G. and the final S.G.

Initial	35
Final	0
	35

LOOK BEFORE YOU LEAP

Divide by 7·36 to obtain alcohol (by volume): 4·7%.

A strong beer probably won't ferment right down to zero. The figure to be divided is the difference between the initial and final S.G.

Initial	60
Final	9
	51

Divide by 7·36. Alcohol 6·9%.

These figures are not quite accurate if taken at the bottling stage, because some further fermentation takes place in the bottle. Consequently if greater accuracy is wanted, test the beer at the time you drink it.

Finally, the hydrometer is the best judge of the time to bottle. If the beer is still over 10, bottling is futile. If the bottles don't burst, the beer will be too frisky to pour. Most of it will go on the walls and floors. Only an inch of beer and about five inches of froth will get into your glass.

Although the hydrometer doesn't measure yeast content, intelligent use of the instrument enables the beer maker to get as much or as little yeast into the bottle as he wishes. When the reading is still 10, the yeast has not yet settled. A great deal of it is still working up and down in the liquid in the business of fermentation. The beer is therefore not racked until the yeast settles, the whole purpose of racking being to leave the yeast and other sediment behind. On the other hand, if the reading sinks to zero and the beer isn't racked for a day or two after that, the beer falls clear, practically all the yeast settles and no gas will be formed in the bottle.

Now let's get back to the excise system of fixing beer duty.

Not surprisingly, it's based on the strength of beer. The stronger the beer, the more duty has to be paid.

Since alcohol content is normally determined by the above methods rather than by chemical analysis, the relevant figures are the initial and final gravity figures. In practice, since brewers can be trusted to conduct the fermentation with complete efficiency, the only figure which matters is the initial S.G. This figure determines the duty to be paid on the batch of beer.

This system tends to reduce the strength of beer. About the turn of the century, average initial S.G. was over 50. At the present time it is about 35. This means that beer has not much more than half the strength it used to have. How this came about, in general, is quite simple: every time the duty was raised, as it has been many times, the brewer was faced with the choice of putting up prices or weakening the beer. The second course had the double advantage of saving materials (malt and hops) and saving duty. Sometimes one course was chosen, sometimes the other. But over the years the general tendency has been to weaken the beer considerably.

At the present time, with high duty payable and no prospect of any reduction, ever, the brewer finds himself in a tricky position. At very little extra cost in materials he could produce a much better beer. But the duty would rise. Customers would have to pay not only for the extra materials but also duty. It would be a double rise.

The brewer therefore tries to find the best compromise in price, quantity and quality. Bulk beers are generally as economical as he can make them, not strong and therefore less heavily taxed. Stronger beers are sold in small bottles. The customer doesn't escape the higher rate of duty, but he doesn't have his face rubbed in it. He gets a small glass of strong ale instead of a big glass of weak ale at about the same price.

I have been using the description 'weak ale' deliberately, with no derogatory intention, merely a desire to be accurate. Naturally no brewer has ever issued anything called weak ale, or wishy-washy ale, or low-alcohol beer. Beer is supposed to be a man's drink, a manly drink, a virile drink. It's often called strong when it isn't. It's never called weak even when it is. Yet one can say without shame that one likes weak tea. The trouble is that the various euphemisms which have been employed—light ale, pale ale, mild ale—also apply to qualities other than strength. Pale ale, naturally, is pale in colour. The colour is no guide whatever to its potency. You can make $2\frac{1}{2}\%$ (alcohol percentage) pale ale or 10% pale ale. Similarly, dark beer is not necessarily strong. Even apparently heavy beer is not necessarily strong. Then beer can be mild in the sense that it lacks bitterness, yet very potent. To avoid misunderstanding, therefore, the words light, pale, mild and bitter are used here of colour and taste, and the words weak and strong of alcohol content.

Although recipes are unnecessary and the beer maker is advised rather to work on the general principles already stated, some people aren't happy unless they have lists of ingredients to keep them right and detailed step-by-step instructions. The instructions are given in Chapter Eight. A few basic recipes are given here.

Why separate them? Because beer making is not like cooking. In cooking, method and materials are virtually inseparable. Instructions for baking a pie simply would not do for baking fish. No experienced chef would dream of giving general instructions for grilling, to be applied indiscriminately to steak, fish and toast.

In making beer, general know-how is more important than specialized know-how. The ingredients in a recipe, written down or evolved in the brewer's head as he goes along, should *tell* him what to do with them. Malt must be mashed. It's no use tipping it into boiling water and stewing it. Hops must be boiled. Yeast must be added to the cooled wort. After fermentation, the beer must .be racked. All these things are general. It would be a waste of space, and, worse, a waste of your time if for twenty recipes twenty methods were given (or repeated). There are only about three or four methods the home brewer can use, and each of them can be applied to any recipe. After two or three brews he will have established for himself the most convenient method in his circumstances. He may never need to change it.

In the following recipes, dried or liquid malt extract can be substituted for malt, in the same quantities. This doesn't mean that in all cases the result will be the same—it won't be. It merely means that the recipe will still work. Obviously, the method may be different. Hop extract can be substituted for hops, but if it is, the result will certainly be quite different and no guidance can be given on quantities. There are at least six varieties of hop extract obtainable which don't look alike or smell alike, and the suppliers' recommendations alone, without experiment, show that the hop content varies considerably.

(*To make five gallons*)

LIGHT ALE (A weak, mild beer)

63

LOOK BEFORE YOU LEAP

2 lb. pale malt
2 lb. sugar
2 oz. hops
Sedimentary ale yeast
1 teaspoon salt
2–3 teaspoons citric acid

PALE ALE (An average pale ale)
3 lb. pale malt
2 lb. sugar
3 oz. hops
Yeast
1 teaspoon salt
2–3 teaspoons citric acid

PALE ALE (Stronger and more bitter)
3 lb. pale malt
½ lb. maize (flaked or broken)
3 lb. sugar
4 oz. hops
Yeast
2 teaspoons salt
3 teaspoons citric acid

BROWN ALE (Dark but weak)
1 lb. crystal malt
1 lb. black malt
1 lb. sugar
2 oz. hops
1 lb. treacle
Yeast

LOOK BEFORE YOU LEAP

1 teaspoon salt
2–3 teaspoons citric acid

BROWN ALE (Stronger and more bitter)
3 lb. crystal malt
1 lb. black malt
2 lb. sugar
4 oz. hops
1 lb. treacle
Yeast
2 teaspoons salt
3 teaspoons citric acid

MILD BEER (Mild but not weak)
3 lb. crystal malt
½ lb. black malt
½ lb. maize
3 lb. sugar
3 oz. hops
Yeast
1 teaspoon salt
3 teaspoons citric acid

BITTER BEER (Handle with care)
5 lb. crystal malt
1 lb. maize
4 lb. sugar
6–8 oz. hops
Hardening treatment if soft water used
(Burton crystals or 3 teaspoons gypsum)

LOOK BEFORE YOU LEAP

Yeast
3 teaspoons citric acid

LAGER (Weak)
3 lb. pale malt
1 lb. sugar
2 oz. hops
Softening treatment if hard water used
Yeast
1 teaspoon salt
2 teaspoons citric acid

LAGER (Strong)
6 lb. pale malt
2 lb. maize
3 oz. hops
Softening treatment if hard water used
Yeast
1 teaspoon salt
3 teaspoons citric acid

STOUT (Mild, sweet and harmless, not a true stout)
2 lb. patent black malt
2 lb. pale malt
1 lb. lactose
2 oz. hops
Softening treatment
Yeast
2 teaspoons salt
2 teaspoons citric acid

STOUT (MILK STOUT) (Still sweet but stronger)
>   2 lb. patent black malt
>   2 lb. pale malt
>   1 lb. sugar
>   1 lb. treacle
>   1 lb. lactose
>   3 oz. hops
>   Softening treatment
>   Yeast
>   2 teaspoons salt
>   3 teaspoons citric acid

OATMEAL STOUT (Bitter for a stout, and strong)
>   3 lb. patent black malt
>   2 lb. pale malt
>   ½ lb. oatmeal
>   2 lb. sugar
>   1 lb. treacle
>   5 oz. hops
>   Softening treatment
>   Yeast
>   2 teaspoons salt
>   3 teaspoons citric acid

STRONG ALE (And it is)
>   4 lb. crystal malt
>   1 lb. black malt
>   1 lb. maize
>   4 lb. brown sugar
>   ½ lb. treacle

LOOK BEFORE YOU LEAP

6–8 oz. hops
Hardening treatment
Yeast
3 teaspoons citric acid

CHAPTER VII

What's in store

> But if at the Church they would give us some ale,
> And a pleasant fire our souls to regale,
> We'd sing and we'd play all the livelong day,
> Nor ever once wish from the Church to stray.
>
> WILLIAM BLAKE, *Songs of Experience*

Basic things like malt, sugar, hops and water have already been considered in some detail. These are the essential ingredients. There are many other things which can be added to beer, or used in the production of beer.

If you write to one of the main suppliers and ask for their catalogue, you will receive a list of perhaps twenty pages, usually more concerned with wine than beer making. Although most such catalogues are reasonably informative, one can't expect every item to be described in detail, with its function.

This chapter is intended as a guide to the main items available.

The various forms of malt should not be a source of much difficulty. Grain malt must of course be mashed at a temperature considerably below boiling-point. Extracts, liquid or dried, don't need mashing unless the diastase in them is to be used to break down the starch in extra grain. Prices vary: naturally this affects every beer maker's choice.

It is impossible to give much guidance on hops or hop extract, because usually a supplier simply lists 'dried hops' and leaves it at that, and 'hop extract, sufficient for x gallons', and the price. I don't want to recommend any particular brand for several reasons, one of which is that products change frequently. After one writes down and prints in permanent form that Hogg's Pork Pies are the best in the world, they are quite liable to change the pastry, the pork and the cooking methods with the result that Hogg's Pork Pies become very nearly the worst in the world.

One variety of hop extract which at present might be rated the best is black and treacly and comes in tins. Another good one, in small bottles, is so black and thick that it doesn't pour at all, and is difficult to mix with water. The use of warm water to dissolve it is obligatory. Others are thin green-brown liquids liable to throw vegetable deposits.

We all find a variety that suits us and usually, if we're sensible, stick to it. *De predicamento tuo non curo . . Jack.*

In addition to hop extract, oil of hops is available. This is excellent for use at the penultimate stage, the stage of bottling, and it really does restore much of the aromatic oil that has been lost.

Before further consideration of ingredients, something which is not an ingredient yet is just as basic should be considered. This is the siphon.

In the description of methods in the first chapter, a description which, it must now be obvious, was beer making reduced to its most elementary form, ignoring all the finer points, the racking process amounted merely to pouring the beer from one container to another as carefully as possible. This is only a makeshift method. No matter how carefully it is done, the sediment must be stirred up to some extent and more sediment than is desirable is carried forward.

The only way to rack efficiently is to draw off the beer without disturbing the sediment, stopping the operation well above the yeast and other matter which should be left behind.

There are two simple ways of doing this, the use of a cask or jar with a tap set above sediment level, or siphoning. The use of casks and jars is discussed later. However, for best results you must have an efficient siphon even if you never dream of buying a special tap jar or oak cask for beer making. The siphon, short of this, is as basic as the malt and hops you use.

You can make a perfectly good siphon with about four feet of plastic or rubber tubing. This is tied to a clean stick (bamboo is excellent) a little longer than the depth of your fermenting vessel, with one end about three inches short of the end of the stick. When racking is necessary, the fermenting vessel is carefully lifted above the level of the container into which the beer is to be racked—better still, it was there all the time—and the stick with the tube is stood in the beer. It is then only necessary to suck the free end steadily until the beer comes, insert it in the second container, and the clear beer flows freely. If it's not clear, but thick and milky, the tube is set too low on the stick and yeast is being drawn through. When the level sinks to the tube opening, air gets in and the flow stops.

Preferable to this is the use of a siphon designed and made for the job. All the suppliers stock several varieties. These siphons are basically similar to the makeshift one described, but are more convenient to use. Some have a tap at the free end. Others are so constructed that instead of having to suck beer which doesn't at this stage taste like beer at all, you merely have to blow to start the siphon. All are preferable to the makeshift siphon in that the tube is turned up so that instead of the suction being toward the bottom, possibly attracting some yeast, the beer enters the siphon from above.

All the recipes given call for the use of citric acid.

In all fermentation, in addition to sugar, some acid should be present. This helps to keep the fermentation stable; in the total absence of acid, unpleasant flavours may occur. All fruit contains acid, except possibly some dried fruits like dates and figs. The home wine maker therefore doesn't always have to add acid. In the ordinary sweet wort, however, no acid is present and it has to be supplied.

Citric acid, though now entirely synthetic, is equivalent to lemon juice. Lemon juice can still be used, but citric acid obtainable cheaply from a chemist will do perfectly well. Tartaric acid can be used instead or as well, but *not* acetic acid.

Citric acid has a beneficial effect on the fermentation, which will go better and faster with than without it. The quantities are not critical. Even a very small quantity will probably prevent bad flavours, and quite a large quantity would have to be present before the taste of the beer would be affected. Anyway, the taste, roughly that of lemonade, goes well with a carbonated drink and it wouldn't be a serious matter if you could detect it.

Tannin is also a very desirable ingredient in beer. There is some in hops but not enough.

Tannin, very bitter in taste, has a wonderful effect on the clarification of beer. It is obtainable as grape tannin, a copper-coloured powder very economical in use, since only a tiny quantity is needed in a five-gallon brew. Probably preferable, cheaper and simpler is the use of cold tea. A few tablespoons contain enough tannin, yet half a gallon would not be too much. Thus, as with citric acid, the possibility of error is easily eliminated.

Other writers on beer making demand in every brew the use of yeast food or yeast nutrient.

Any kind of yeast needs sustenance before it can grow, and this is very important because it grows first and then gets to work. For various excellent reasons we invariably add less yeast than necessary to the cooled wort rather than more. The yeast first grows, which it can do with astonishing rapidity, and then starts fermenting. Although yeast uses some of the sugar simply as food, sugar alone is not a complete food for any of the varieties of yeast used in making wine or beer. They need rather the vegetable matter present in all liquids made from fruit, flowers or grain. It is therefore common, if not obligatory, to provide yeast used in amateur wine making with a certain amount of proprietary yeast food containing tartaric and citric acid, ammonium and magnesium sulphate and potassium phosphate. Some of these ingredients, incidentally, are used in chemical fertilizers, and for approximately the same reason. They aid vegetable growth, and the yeast reproduction cycle is also vegetable-based. Remove *all* vegetable matter from a liquid, sugar it and add yeast, and it's doubtful if a fermentation can start. It will certainly soon be over, with most of the sugar unconverted.

This is why yeast nutrient is added in wine making. However, there is no better yeast nutrient than malt. Malt extract, indeed, is one of the best media in which to grow yeast. Therefore, far from being 'essential' in a beer brew, yeast nutrient is often quite unnecessary and never even desirable, except in weak brews or in the dead of winter.

Use yeast nutrient if you like. By all means use it when the strain of yeast used is inactive and needs a shot in the arm. Use it when you want a quick, vigorous, complete fermentation. Have some on hand always, because there are times in the best-regulated home breweries when a fermentation hangs fire before starting, or sticks after starting, or refuses to work to completion.

But yeast nutrient is never essential when you're using malt, the best yeast nutrient there is.

Most of the other items in the suppliers' catalogues can be dealt with briefly.

Heading liquid is exactly what it claims to be, a concentrate which, added to beer before bottling, will ensure a fine head of froth on the top of every pint. It is cheap and highly efficient. The question is: do you need it? If you find your bottles pop in an uninhibited manner when you open them and you have to pour carefully, tilting the glass and gradually restoring it to the vertical position, heading liquid is not for you. Its use would mean that a pint bottle would supply you with a third of a glass of beer and two-thirds froth. On the other hand, if your beers tend to be flat, or don't retain their head after pouring, heading liquid will be very useful.

Gypsum has been mentioned: for brewers in soft-water areas, hard water is sometimes desirable.

Liquorice stick is used sometimes in the production of dark beers and stout. It supplies colour and a certain foggy sweetness. It is certainly one man's meat and another man's poison. It may be essential to one beer maker, anathema to another.

Yeasts and yeast nutrients take up pages in catalogues. All the beer maker needs is a sedimentary (bottom-working) beer, lager or ale yeast. Cost is immaterial because he need never buy any more. One of the snags about catalogues is that since most of the materials are for wine rather than beer, the yeasts may be mixed up. If in doubt, get a lager yeast, as this *must* be a sedimentary ale yeast. It doesn't matter whether the yeast is in dried or liquid or even tablet form. This is easily dealt with.

Ignore the pages on malic acid, pectozyme, Campden tablets and anti-fermentation solutions. Pay no attention to corks, bungs and plastic seals. These are for wine makers. Airlocks or fermentation locks are essential for the wine maker, optional for the maker of beer. Funnels and strainers are useful, but you can buy perfectly adequate materials at any big store.

Labels for bottles are also optional. Are you going to put a label on every bottle of beer you make? Remember, there are eight pints in a gallon. A five-gallon brew will supply about thirty-two bottles—not, unfortunately, forty. Racking or double-racking will account for the rest. The enthusiastic tyro might well put labels on his first few brews, but after that. . . .

The only major omission from this brief amble through lists of materials available to the home brewer is the section on fining and priming. This is so tied up with method that the subject is left to the next chapter.

CHAPTER VIII

Methods

I will make it felony to drink small beer.
SHAKESPEARE, *Henry VI*, Part II.

Make weak beer by all means—but never small beer. Small beer, in the old days, was the brew from the leftovers, the nearly spent grain and, if used, hops. Of course it must have been a thin, pale shadow of the main brew. Hence the derogatory idiom which has passed into the language—'very small beer'. But small beer was worse than merely a weak beer. It was a beer which could not have been good because it was made from wort residue after all the chemical processes described earlier had taken place.

Generous squires undoubtedly added fresh grain to the second boiling, with the result that the beer wasn't small at all. In the ordinary way, however, the wort residue is useful only as fertilizer.

This is merely a roundabout way of getting into, at last, a detailed consideration of methods available to the home brewer.

What has gone before should make brewing methods, in theory, a familiar story. Malt must be mashed, that is, the starch must be converted at 150° F. Hops must be added—boiled with the wort after mashing, boiled separately, or supplied in the form of hop extract. The wort must be strained in some way. After cooling it must be pitched with yeast, and after the necessary period of fermentation it must be racked at least once. Then it must be bottled in bottles capable of retaining considerable pressure.

There's no getting around any of this, except by the use of instant wort as described in the first chapter. The simple boiling of packaged malt and hops described at the same time, it must now be obvious, is a compromise, a way in which someone who doesn't understand what he's doing can make a passable beer fairly simply. Don't blame the suppliers. They print brief instructions on a label which will enable an average do-it-yourself man to accomplish a reasonable product without being called upon to comprehend the subtleties of the operation. In the same way, a DIY man who buys a kit of parts expects to be told to join A to B and X to Y, and how. He doesn't expect to have to read through ten closely-printed pages telling him why. These packages are made up and the brief instructions printed in the hope that as the malt is gradually taken to boiling point some enzyme activity will take place to convert the starch and some of the desirable contributions of the hops will get into the wort.

The home brewer who does understand the subtleties has to figure out a way of getting the best from his materials in his particular circumstances.

The easiest way to make beer, short of instant beer, is by the use of malt extract, dry or liquid. If extra grain is not used, there is no need to mash at all. The malt extract can be boiled with hops, or simply dissolved in hot water, hop extract being added later. Alternatively, the hops may be boiled separately and the hot liquid can be poured over the malt extract to dissolve it. Still another way is to ferment the wort without hops and add hop liquor or hop extract either near the end of fermentation or after the first racking.

Some salt should be added in any case, whether the water is hard or soft. It can't do any harm, in small quantities, and it may do a lot of good. If the water is hard, particularly, it should be introduced right at the beginning.

Citric acid is not needed until fermentation starts. It should be added just before the yeast. Tannin can be added at the same time.

Sugar can be introduced at any time, but the obvious stage is just after straining. The wort is sweet and sticky anyway. If it's made too sweet and sticky, the straining operation, however it is carried out, will be slower, less efficient and more messy. Household sugar contains nothing which must be kept back from the fermenting vessel. It dissolves quickly and easily in hot liquid and slowly and incompletely in cold water. Pouring hot wort into sugar is a simple way of integrating the liquid to be fermented. It is preferable for this to be done a stage before the fermentation vessel itself, to ensure that no undissolved sugar is lying at the bottom when the yeast is introduced.

Yeast lives on sugar and goes to work madly on sugar, but a surfeit can be deadly. Even vigorous beer yeasts can be turned lethargic when they drop into a thick crust of undissolved sugar. They can even be killed outright—and with yeast, that's saying something. All sugar poured into the vessel in which fermentation is to take place should therefore be completely dissolved, not merely in suspension and liable to settle later.

Water treatment, if any, should be done early in the proceedings. The instructions supplied will make this clear.

Finally, if hops are merely to be added early or late as flavouring rather than as a part of the chemical process of brewing (and this is usually the case when malt extract is used), the best way to deal with them is to boil them quickly in a small quantity of water in a small closed saucepan for not more than half an hour, cool the saucepan in a basin of cold water and strain the liquid.

These are some guiding principles for beer made with malt extract with and without extra grain and with hops or hop extract :

Malt extract, hop extract, no extra grain, no sugar:
Pour boiling water over the malt extract and salt and stir until dissolved. After cooling, add citric acid, tannin, yeast. Cover. When fermentation is complete, siphon off beer, add hop extract, mix thoroughly. Leave in covered container for 24 hours. Siphon again. Bottle in pint screwtop bottles, adding to each half a teaspoon of sugar. Leave upright for 7–14 days.

Malt extract, hop extract, extra grain, no sugar:
The very presence of extra grain means mashing is necessary. Otherwise you might as well throw the grain away. The method is the same as before, except that the diastase in the malt extract must be given a chance to convert the extra starch, and the wort must then be boiled to stop enzyme activity. So the process is: malt extract and grain are brought to 150° F.

80

and kept there for two hours. Then the liquor is strained. Everything else as before.

Malt extract differs, and some varieties may have been treated with preservatives or boiled. Malt extract intended for brewing should therefore be used. Once the enzymes have been killed, you can't expect them to rise from the grave to convert starch for you.

Malt extract, hop extract, extra grain, extra sugar:
The only extra step is to dissolve the sugar and make sure it's really dissolved. Naturally it must go in before fermentation, so the sugar is dissolved in the hot wort after straining.

A small but important extra stage has been slipped in: add to each bottle half a teaspoon of sugar. This is what is meant by the word *priming*.

If beer is bottled too soon, it won't need priming. It will probably burst the bottle anyway. Beer should be bottled just as yeast activity ceases, and just enough sugar is added to enable gas to be formed without starting a major secondary fermentation.

Beginners are liable to bottle too soon anyway. Many years ago, when home brewing without a licence was illegal and I knew nothing about the process myself, being a law-abiding citizen, I tasted beer made by a friend. His crime against the laws of the land was in the event slight compared with his crime against beer. The liquid (one couldn't call it beer) was flat, sweet and sickly. It was agreed that the experiment might be worth repeating with far less sugar. In fact, what had happened was that virtually no primary fermentation was allowed for and the liquid which was bottled was sweet wort rather than beer. There was so much sugar and so little yeast—and the yeast present was in a weakened condition owing to the excess of sugar, absence of other nourishment and absence of air—that little or no further fermentation took place. In any case, not enough time was allowed for this. In such extreme conditions, which should never occur at all, it could take six or eight weeks for the minute quantities of yeast present in each bottle to recover, grow, and begin to ferment. Then, with no escape for the gas, the bottles would crack one after the other, covering the floor with sticky foam.

This is a good example of the way in which things can go wrong when a would-be brewer doesn't know what he's doing. The case is worth examining because, inverted, it shows how beer *should* be made, and particularly how the priming should be carried out.

I don't know how my friend obtained the wort in the first place, and he wouldn't remember now, but it's safe to assume he put malt, hops, sugar and water together in a pot and boiled the lot for some considerable time. There was no mashing. Heated to boiling point as quickly as possible, the malt passed in a matter of seconds through the critical range in which the vital enzyme activity should have taken place. This meant that the starch remained unconverted and later could not ferment. Excessive heat kills off pretty well all malt activity, and about 75% of the potential of the malt must have been thrown away. As for the hops, long boiling with no later additions destroys most of what we particularly want to preserve. So in this brew far more was thrown away after the wort was strained than had succeeded in getting into the wort.

The sugar, on the other hand, all went through.

Probably baker's yeast was used. The beer was left for a

short time, perhaps overnight, and then bottled. In this time it's unlikely the yeast had got to work. Unless made active beforehand, even the most vigorous yeasts tend to lie quiescent for a while, getting used to their new environment and growing.

Consequently when the beer was bottled the yeast was still largely inactive. Most of it went into two or three bottles, the others being virtually without yeast.

Specific gravity of the bottled beer must have been at least 35. And even weeks later, it remained sweet and nasty. This is not the most likely thing to happen in the circumstances described (did my friend, by any chance, *boil* the yeast with the malt and hops?) Beer bottled at 35 with yeast in an active condition could burst every single bottle within an hour or two. But then, if the yeast was active, the condition of the beer would be such that no one would dream of bottling it. This, the miracle of yeast, has to be seen to be comprehended. Sweet wort in a bucket, after yeast is added, can be as flat and still as a glass of water poured the day before. Yet the few hours later, with no further addition, it can be writhing and foaming, popping and fizzing so steadily that you look out to see if what you're hearing is rain on the roof.

Priming can't be done casually and carelessly, because on the condition of the beer at the time, on the amount of sugar added and the time after this the beer is left before drinking depends the quality of the beer you finally drink. Flat beer is useless, and so is too frisky beer. In other brewing processes (except mashing), you are allowed any amount of latitude. But here you have to hit the bullseye.

To complicate the matter, as if it were not complicated enough, you don't want to make beer which must be drunk at a particular time on a particular day, because before this it will be too flat and afterwards it will be too gassy. One solution, and a good one, is the use of a hydrometer. Medium and weak beers should never be bottled until the S.G. has dropped to about 3. Heavier beers probably won't drop as low as this, and may have to be bottled at about 10. It will be found with these beers that the S.G. never does drop very low, and can still be about 5 when the beer is drunk.

If grain malt is used, the process can't be as simple as with extract.

First every home brewer should consider what is to be his basic method of extraction. The main possibilities are:

1. Ingredients mashed and boiled in a pot on electric or gas cooker.
2. Ingredients mashed by use of an immersion heater, then boiled on cooker.
3. Mashing and boiling in electric or gas copper boiler.

In the first case you will have to get rid of spent hops and malt by straining through muslin or a coarser cloth. No false-bottom method is practicable for a pot on a cooker. Alternatively, some of the ingredients, particularly hops, can be put in a muslin bag before boiling, thus avoiding the necessity to strain later.

In the second case you need an immersion heater similar to those used in fish tanks containing tropical fish. They are not expensive, unless you want one with an adjustable thermostat. Wine-making suppliers stock several varieties. If you use an immersion heater, you can easily fix up a false-bottom masher by using a small plastic bucket within a larger one. A highly efficient set-up, if you become enthusiastic and expense becomes secondary, is a plastic bucket with lid and drilled bottom used with immersion heater inside an oak or plastic tub fermenter with tap. It would not be difficult to make such equipment yourself, starting with two plastic containers. The smaller has to have about 100 small holes in the bottom, a simple matter if you possess an electric drill, and if you don't you must know someone who does. Fitting a plastic tap in the side of the larger container is only a little more difficult. This tap need not be particularly efficient, as would be necessary if liquid were to be stored in the container for long periods. Unlike other taps, this one should be set right at the bottom of the container. It's not in this case a matter of drawing off liquid and leaving the sediment behind, but of draining the container completely.

In the third case the tap is already there, and all that is necessary is a false bottom in the boiler to keep back the grain and hops. If you are fortunate enough to possess a suitable boiler it is worth the expense of having a proper false bottom made.

If a boiler is used, it should naturally be clean. Metal contamination can be serious in wine making, but when beer is mashed and boiled in a metal container the only precaution to be taken is to keep all acid out of the wort.

Malt, hops, no extra grain, no sugar: Bring the water to about 150° F., and pour in the malt, lightly crushed. Keep at this temperature for at least two hours. Then either strain or add the hops, take the temperature to boiling point, and boil for an hour, adding fresh hops in the last few minutes. Strain, cool.

If this is done in a pot, there is nothing further you can do. If an immersion heater is used, the wort is strained after mashing and hopping proceeds as before.

If it's all done in a boiler, you need scarcely do more than keep an eye on things.

Malt, hops, extra grain, sugar: The extra grain makes no difference whatever to the method, since the malt has to be mashed anyway. The only time when the addition of grain affects the method is when malt extract is used. Malt extract (a suitable variety) doesn't need mashing, but it's still capable of converting some starch in grains such as maize, rice, barley, wheat and oatmeal.

As for the sugar, it certainly shouldn't be included before straining, since a thick syrup is obviously very hard to strain, and messy besides. If it's put into the fermenting vessel and the sweet wort is poured over it hot, it can quite easily be dissolved then.

When there's a tap somewhere in the production line, extraction is simpler and more efficient. Drawing off liquid and returning it through the mash helps mixing and extraction. Sparging can also be done quite easily. Sparging is sprinkling hot water on the mash, preferably with a watering can, but it can easily be done through a sieve. This extracts anything of value which remains.

Fermentation has been mentioned again and again. Although the most important process, it's the easiest for the brewer, because he does virtually nothing about it. There's nothing he *can* do about it.

When the wort is cool, it is finally adjusted for specific gravity, acidity, colour and so on, and the yeast is added. The container is then closed, and that's that. There's no need to keep an eye on fermentation, because if the work has been done properly up to this point and if the temperature isn't too low, the fermentation must be satisfactory. All you have to do is select the moment for racking, preferably with a hydrometer, rack, let the beer settle, rack again, prime and bottle.

CHAPTER IX

Containers

The heart which grief hath cankered
Hath one unfailing remedy—the Tankard.

C. S. CALVERLEY

W hen anyone blithely brews a few gallons of beer
as an experiment, possibly for the first and last
time, he is not likely, nor would he be wise, to buy
a lot of special equipment and materials. If at least one large
glass or plastic container is available, it may not be necessary
to buy anything more than a tin of instant wort and beer
yeast, or malt and hop extract and yeast.

Past the initial stage, the home brewer is not merely ready
but eager to use anything which will improve his beer or
make brewing more convenient.

There are certainly more convenient ways of making beer
than by the use of a plastic dustbin.

A large plastic carboy with a tap set at the right place is a
very useful thing to have. Empty, these are light and easily
cleaned. They can be swilled out easily, washed with detergent
outside and in, sterilized. Even if left empty for long periods
they can quickly and safely be restored to active life, unlike
casks.

CONTAINERS

Plastic bags and semi-rigid carboys, supported by cardboard, wooden or metal frames, although quite capable of producing good beer, are not at all convenient. People starting home brewing commonly buy cheap containers and later regret it. They wish the 30s. or so spent on an inferior fermenting vessel had gone towards the purchase of something much better.

Let's assume for a moment that money is no object, and draw up a list of the best home-brewing equipment, both for quality and ease of handling.

Top of the list is a good 5–6 gallon oak cask, new or made from sherry casks.

Casks are 'of little use' in home brewing, says one authority (to be fair, he adds that this is because of the difficulty of keeping them clean, and because finished beer kept in casks soon goes flat). Well, it depends how you use them. Nothing, but nothing, will ferment as well in anything else as it does in an oak cask. True, the advantages are greater in the case of wine, which is why oak casks have had such a long innings and are not out yet. But beer, too, can benefit greatly from being fermented in oak. The oak itself contains tannin, and a cask allows a fermenting liquid to breathe as nothing else does. Plastic and stone containers, while they may subtract nothing from a fermentation, add nothing either. Only oak does this.

Personally, I never ferment beer in anything but a cask, having tried all the other possibilities. And anyway, where is the difficulty? We're discussing ideal methods. Ideally, then, there should be constant production, say once a week. The cask is therefore constantly full of fermenting wort. It never dries out and it never goes bad. It is never used for storing beer.

89

CONTAINERS

A three-gallon cask, which isn't much use for anything else, is excellent for the production of beer. But many home brewers make five or six gallons a week (cost not much over 10s.) without finding the supply outstripping the demand. They don't drink it all themselves. They get help. So a five-gallon oak cask is kept in constant production. At the end of the week the beer is racked into smaller containers (plastic casks, also with taps, are excellent for this). The process couldn't be simpler; it's only a matter of turning a tap, and preventing overflowing. When the cask is empty, it is no longer heavy and can be swilled out quickly and easily with a hose at the back door. It doesn't have to be sterilized and only occasionally is a thorough cleaning job desirable. Hot water is used then, and many cold washes under pressure. The yeast slime in the cask is dislodged by rocking the cask.

The barrel is put back in place and filled with the new wort, which can be hot. Topping up is done with a hose. Yeast and anything else necessary are added when the wort is cool, a fermentation lock is inserted, and the cask can be forgotten for another week.

Meantime, the beer in the plastic tap jars is left for twenty-four hours. Bottling is simple apart from the necessary priming. The easiest way to deal with this is to use an eye-dropper squirt and syrup of predetermined S.G. so that one complete, unmeasured squirt is right for the capacity of the bottles used. Each bottle gets a squirt and is then filled from the tap. What could be quicker and less messy? At the end of the operation, the plastic jars are rinsed two or three times and left for a week. They are then rinsed again and the procedure is as before.

For this method, the best and simplest I know, you need a

five-gallon oak cask with tap, bored bung and fermentation lock, two two-gallon plastic casks and a rubber hose of suitable length fitting the tap or taps which must be used. Nominal two-gallon plastic casks invariably hold more, up to 2½ gallons. And you lose some of the capacity of the cask in sediment. The two plastic casks will therefore take all the clear beer from the oak cask.

If hop extract is used, it is poured into the plastic casks just before they are filled. The extract will thus be mixed thoroughly with the ale.

This arrangement produces excellent beer, and the ultimate cost is negligible. The very first five-gallon brew shows a saving equal to the cost of the five-gallon cask.

Prices vary. A five-gallon oak cask costs between £2 and £4. Say £3, and five gallons of beer cost 12s. 6d. to make. You get about 32 pints. Cost per pint, 2s. 3d. How much does a pint cost in your local?

But after this, the cask is yours. The next brew costs just 12s. 6d. Cost per pint, less than 5d.

The two two-gallon plastic casks have not yet been allowed for. These cost about £1 each. The saving on two brews will cover the whole outlay.

If beer is not made regularly, oak casks may indeed be hard to keep fresh. The next best thing is to use stoneware tap jars, which are not at all difficult to keep clean. These are no cheaper than oak casks, and usually the largest size contains four gallons, not five. However, they are tap jars, and therefore racking is simple and efficient.

Stoneware or plastic tap jars, if they have an efficient seal, can also be used for storing beer—with certain advantages and disadvantages.

If you fill a tap jar with water, screw down the lid tight and try to pour a pint, the water will gush freely for a second or two and then die to a thin trickle. If it doesn't, the screwtop isn't sealing properly. You can't pour liquid from any vessel unless air can freely flow in to compensate for the volume lost. Turn a full bottle upside down and see it gulp madly.

But if you fill a tap jar with beer, primed if necessary, pressure builds up in the liquid and in the air space at the top. When you turn the tap some days later, the beer comes out under pressure. Gas escaping into the free space at the top equalizes the lost pressure.

A tap jar can therefore be used for dispensing beer, and to some home brewers this is the ultimate in luxurious living. Beer on tap. . . .

The jar can't be emptied in this way, however. After a while the pressure will fail or the beer will become cloudy. The jar should then either be topped up, primed and left to mature again or the beer should be bottled.

Many variations are possible. If fermentation is in an oak cask the beer can be run into ordinary glass jars without taps and siphoned the next day. Or beer fermented in a plastic dustbin can be siphoned into plastic tap jars.

It should never be forgotten, however, that taps set low in any container, open or closed, greatly simplify the various brewing, maturing and bottling operations. The siphon which is placed in a large container and sucked or blown until the liquor flows is all that is necessary for efficient racking, but it is never as satisfactory as a simple tap.

CONTAINERS

Remember that taps must be wood or plastic. Metal, in the initial stages of mashing and boiling, probably won't do any harm. There is no acid present to eat it away and allow minute, yet dangerous, deposits to get into the wort. Later, during fermentation, maturing or storing, not only is acid present but it is given relatively long periods to get to work on any metal which may be around. No fermenting liquid should ever be in contact with metal.

Glass is quite indifferent to all the acids encountered in brewing, although even glass must be considered a potential enemy when there is the slightest possiblity of acetic acid contamination. A vinegar bottle, scalded, sterilized and washed again and again may still spoil beer or wine poured into it. This is a minor consideration. No wine or beer maker would be likely to use vinegar bottles when others are so readily available.

The snag about glass is the difficulty of fixing taps in it.

Even the modest home brewer will soon find slow methods irksome, and will be glad to make any reorganization in procedure which cuts down the time required for racking and bottling. Racking five gallons by siphon into gallon jars is an operation which must be supervised the whole time. Even when you merely go to the door or answer the telephone, you're liable to be delayed the few extra seconds it takes for the jar to overflow and beer to swamp the floor—and a nasty sticky mess it makes. Also, if you pick up a newspaper for a moment or glance at a television programme, it's easy to become absorbed . . . and later find four gallons of beer flooding the house. It's astonishing how little beer on the floor is needed to give the impression of a new Deluge. Half a gallon seems like six.

CONTAINERS

The ideal method is to arrange the racking so that this can't happen, for instance racking from a tap jar or cask on an upper shelf into a tap jar of the same capacity on a lower shelf. There is no need to move the lower jar. It can be stoppered and left until bottling time, the upper jar or cask being cleaned meantime and filled with the new wort. Later, primed bottles can be filled direct from the lower jar *in situ*.

Going to some trouble and expense to arrange such a set-up repays handsome dividends whenever racking and bottling time comes along.

One reason why work study is often resented in factories is because all intelligent workers who have been at the job for some time have already figured out a system which is reasonably efficient and which suits them. Dull, boring operations are cut out altogether where possible, and in other cases reduced to the minimum expenditure of time and effort. Interesting or absolutely vital stages are given the attention they deserve. A worker who has to sit still most of the time welcomes a regular opportunity to stretch his legs, and won't be at all enthusiastic when the work-study expert finds a way to cut out a periodic stroll from point A to point B and back. Very often the skilled although uneducated worker is right and the expert is wrong. The apparently inefficient method is in the end safer, more efficient and more satisfying temperamentally.

The home brewer should apply work-study thinking for himself. Even a simple matter like cleaning bottles becomes worthy of a little thought when it's not a question of cleaning one bottle, but fifty. It takes a long time to pour water in a bottle, shake it, pour out the water, rinse it, clean the stopper —and then repeat the operation forty-nine times. Yet bottles

CONTAINERS

must be clean, obviously, and the best time to do the cleaning, the final cleaning at any rate, is immediately before they are to be filled.

The kitchen is bound to have two taps, possibly four. An efficient and reasonably quick method is to have all four taps running slowly at a little more than a drip, and put the bottles first under Cold 1, then Cold 2, Hot 1 and finally Hot 2. Each bottle, when three-quarters full, is inverted in some kind of stand so that you don't have to wait every time (200 times!) for the water to flow out. In this way the labour consists simply of lifting and shifting bottles in a steady routine. The hot water should not be too hot. Slow filling, however, will lessen the risk of bursting.

By some such method fifty bottles can be cleaned in the time fifteen would need, handled individually.

Casks make the best beer, and casks or jars with taps, stored at appropriate levels, can save up to 80% of the time needed for all operations between boiling and drinking the beer. Are there any other short cuts? Not many, unfortunately. One is to rinse every bottle as it is emptied. The yeast sediment comes away easily then, but if allowed to dry, it cakes and is hard to dislodge.

Priming is another production bottleneck. Sometimes the addition of syrup after the first racking is recommended. If this is done, the beer can be bottled later (from tap jars, this constitutes the second racking) straight into clean bottles. While convenient, this method is not wholly satisfactory. Fresh sugar encourages renewed yeast growth and activity. Beer which has been racked for the first time at exactly the right stage, beginning to clear yet still containing enough

95

yeast for a satisfactory bottle fermentation, can quite easily become cloudy and yeasty again after the addition of sugar, in a more active state than it should be for bottling. And if the beer is primed in bulk immediately before bottling, mixing won't be at all adequate. Clearly the beer can't be stirred or otherwise agitated at this stage—that would mix up in it the yeast which has been allowed to settle. The tendency is for too much sugar to get into some bottles and none at all in others.

Perhaps the easiest way is to bottle by tap and funnel, adding a half teaspoon of sugar or the equivalent in syrup as the bottle is filling.

An apparently simple thing like storing the bottles can be a bit of a headache. Since the yeast is to settle in a firm sediment on the bottom, all bottles must be stored upright at all times. If this isn't done, the sediment forms on the sides and is sure to be dislodged and poured into the glass when the beer is drunk. Leaving the bottles untouched from the moment of bottling to the moment of drinking is ideal, if it can be accomplished. But the bottles have to stand for at least a week and perhaps three. They cannot therefore be placed right away in the bottom of a cocktail cabinet, for instance, because this is required for beer ready to drink, rather than beer which must remain untouched for some considerable time. Successive brews should be used in the order of bottling, and the only way to do this easily and without slip-ups is to store the bottles in a roughly circular manner, so that Brew 7 is not started until Brew 6 is exhausted. Failing the circular method, you're liable to find yourself shifting fifty bottles three or four times before they're finally opened.

Of course, if you have several varieties of beer running together, in order to have a choice of type, labelling may become obligatory. A good plan to avoid confusion is to try to make successive brews distinguishable in colour, if only to know which is which in case of doubt.

Not much need be said about bottles, except that they should be clear screwtops, preferably in pint size.

Commercial beer almost invariably comes in dark bottles, pint (screwtop) or lesser quantities (crown closure), or in cans. This is partly because the colour of beer is affected by light. For the home brewer this is no great matter: the beer is seldom left long enough to be affected at all, and if fading is seen to occur, the beer can be made darker in the first place if desired.

Commercial beer, with a few rare exceptions, has no noticeable sediment. The home brewer's has. To be able to pour perfectly clear, sparkling beer, he must be able to see what he is doing. Through a clear bottle he can see the white trails of yeast stirring during pouring and beginning to meander along the bottle towards the top, and stop pouring just as they reach it, thus ensuring the beer in the glass is virtually free of yeast and at the same time all available clear beer has been poured off. If dark bottles are used, pouring becomes a gamble. If the pourer is too greedy, he doesn't stop in time to check the yeast, a small quantity of which immediately clouds all the beer in the glass, and, far worse, spoils the taste. Excellent food though yeast is, it is bitter and nasty to the taste, and a home-brew connoisseur who inadvertently gets yeast in his pint will either pour it back to settle or pour it down the sink. If the pourer is too cautious, he'll get only about half a pint of beer in the glass, the rest becoming cloudy in the bottle as soon as it is returned to the vertical position.

Clear bottles are therefore the only ones that are of any use. Quart cider bottles (dark) are sometimes recommended, goodness knows why—in addition to the pouring difficulty described, they contain far too much for a pint glass. Unless you propose to drink in litres, quart bottles are useless.

Aerated waters are more and more commonly sold in bottles with metal caps. These differ over the country, but in general they are not as reliable as the ordinary stone or plastic screw stopper with a rubber ring. If a dozen metal-capped bottles are used, nine or ten are later found to have held the pressure adequately, but the others don't fizz on being opened, the gas formed having escaped. Try to get an adequate supply of plain, clear, pint lemonade bottles with substantial screw stoppers and rubber rings, and keep them. When the rubber rings perish, as they will eventually, it is possible to buy more.

Finally, beer must be drunk out of something.

It's wasteful to use glasses which can't take the quantity of clear beer available from each bottle, usually about eighteen ounces. Although partially-poured home-brew bottles can be emptied into a larger vessel and brought back into peak condition by storing again, there are limits—this can be done only once or at most twice, after which the beer won't clear again or won't form gas, even with priming. It can even go bad. The best system is to pour each bottle carefully into a drinking vessel which will contain all the clear beer, and throw the sediment away.

If you use pint bottles, this means pint containers of some kind. These don't have to be clear. The important thing to watch in pouring is the beer inside the bottle. If you like pewter tankards, there is no reason why these should not be used. Plain pint glasses are the most sensible choice, because the sides are straight and relatively long, and consequently even rather frisky beer can be poured gently down the side of a tilted glass, ensuring maximum clarity and quality. Glass tankards with dimpled sides and a handle are becoming more and more popular, and the only slight snag about these is that when the beer is very fizzy probably less of it will get into the glass than when plain pint glasses are used.

Smaller glasses should not be used in the pious hope that more than one can be filled from the same bottle. A gently tilted bottle of home-brewed beer can be emptied to the last half-inch of sediment, but even a half bottle, turned back and then poured into a second glass, will no longer provide clear beer.

The attractive idea of filling a jug of beer is not satisfactory in practice. The beer in the jug may be in first-class condition, but with every second it stands, gas is lost, and when the beer is poured into glasses the froth which is formed won't last long.

If you do want froth to last, use heading liquid.

CHAPTER X

Yeast

Life is mostly froth and bubble.

A. L. GORDON

Yeast is so important in the making of all alcohol that it deserves consideration by itself.

Throughout this book I have specified sedimentary ale yeast and no methods of using top-working yeast have been taken seriously. Yet most commercial beer in this country is made from top-working yeast. And certain other writers on home brewing assume the use of a top yeast.

Frankly, I can't think why.

You can skim yeast if you use open vessels for fermenting, but once beer is bottled you can't skim from the top. You *can* pour off from the top. Now although it's true that top-working yeast eventually does settle, its settling qualities simply cannot compare with those of a yeast which settles from the start, works from the bottom even while extremely active, and forms in quiescence a solid sediment which can easily be left behind in pouring.

Fining has scarcely been mentioned. This is a process of clarifying beer, commonly used in commercial brewing to make a brilliant beer. It has not been described because it simply isn't necessary. Beer made sensibly can't possible require fining. True, it is cloudy during fermentation and for some time after bottling. But if it doesn't clear from the top until you can pour a glass of light or dark beer as clear and sparkling as you can buy in any pub, there's something wrong with your ingredients, water, yeast or methods. These should be corrected. Resorting to fining is treating the symptom and not the disease.

Possibly straining has been inadequate. In brewing we produce a liquid from various solids, and the chance of carrying through solid particles is always present. Starch hazes are not uncommon in beer. If they're present, however, the technique has been imperfect (mashing temperature too high or too low, perhaps, or wrong type of malt).

If your beer is not brilliantly clear, the first things to try are more efficient straining and the addition of more tannin. Don't try to work on the finished beer—the home brewer has to be a fatalist in his recognition that what is done is done and can't be undone. He can't take a particular brew back to the opening stages and start again. At worst, it may have to be thrown away (though no such tragedy need ever occur).

The next brew should have more tannin, either as a powder or in the form of tea.

Home brewing, if it amounts to more than a sporadic experiment, should be a steady, regular, organized operation. And if it is, any disappointments that occur, short of total disaster, can be taken in one's stride.

If the first brews are not entirely satisfactory, and the methods are sound, every beer made can be expected to be better than the last.

YEAST

You start off with containers which are not used to the job in hand. A cask, for instance, won't even hold water until it has been thoroughly soaked for a day or two. Even after that it may be necessary to tighten the bungs and hammer the tap home. The yeast you are using, though the right type, will lack vigour until umpteen generations later. And the quality and exact condition of the yeast used are basic in beer making.

The yeast reproduction cycle makes rabbits appear sterile. Yeast cells, in the right conditions, reproduce within minutes. If yeast in this respect were like elephants, there would never have been any alcohol in the world. Although the original cell becomes exhausted fairly quickly, all the new cells have the same reproductive ability. So yeast doesn't merely reproduce —it explodes.

Beer is anything but delicate, and can be produced by almost any kind of yeast. Bottom yeast is best mainly because, from the very beginning in home brewing, everything leads to an eventual bottle fermentation and the separation of beer from yeast before consumption.

Yeast can be changed in condition, potential, and even in nature by the environment in which it lives. Consider a theoretical case : suppose a yeast which tended to fly about in a fermenting liquid was used (powder yeast). Suppose the next fermentation was induced only by yeast which had settled to the bottom of the fermenting vessel. Suppose this went on and on. . . .

In the end, the powder yeast would be converted into a bottom yeast. The strains which went to the top would be skimmed off. Only the strains which went to the bottom would be encouraged.

102

YEAST

This is how the home brewer refines and re-refines his basic yeast.

The first brew is made by any of the methods described. The beer, after all the processes and conditioning, is drunk. All yeast which remains after fermentation is thrown away.

The yeast for the next fermentation is obtained from the sediment left in the bottles. It is, therefore, yeast which has remained in the beer after first racking, or has grown later, and has settled. Yeast which has not settled cannot be present. The sedimentary yeast starts the next fermentation, and the process is repeated. Every time, only yeast which settles firmly is used for subsequent fermentation.

The natural consequence is that as time goes on the yeast used for brewing is more inclined to settle and more capable of surviving in relatively high alcohol concentrations. It has been bred for this, through thousands of generations.

When you buy beer yeast for the first and last time, it will come as a small bottle of liquid, as a powder, or in tablet form. Although in any of these forms the yeast can be added direct to the wort and will induce fermentation, it may lie several days before fermentation starts and during this time there is a risk that the wort will spoil. In any case, there is no need for this delay.

Mix up the yeast in a strong screwtop bottle with a little malt extract, water and a trace of citric acid. Within twelve, twenty-four or at most forty-eight hours there will be a very vigorous little fermentation going in the bottle. There is serious risk of the bottle bursting, but of course this pilot fermentation should be watched very closely and checked regularly. Every few hours, shake the bottle and unscrew the top. At first nothing will happen. Then the bottle will fizz slightly when opened. Later it will pop loudly and a brown foam will try to shoot out of the bottle, and will succeed if you don't regulate it with the screwtop. Screw stoppers are handy not only because they are a perfect seal, but also because they can be an imperfect seal if desired. When the starter bottle of yeast is blowing off gas violently, you can set the screw stopper carefully so that gas can escape slowly, the stopper becoming a seal again when the pressure drops.

At the stage when you can't afford to shake the bottle any more, when the contents are literally in ferment, the yeast is in excellent condition to start a larger fermentation in the shortest possible time. Pour the whole contents into the cool wort. There is no need to keep back any yeast for the next time.

Some days later, when the beer is racked, a thick creamy sediment will remain in the fermentation vessel. There is no need to keep any of this either. It should all be swilled away and the cask or jar made as clean and fresh as possible.

A second brew can be made simply by pouring the cooled wort into the fermentation vessel without removing the sediment. The old yeast will get to work at once. There is no harm in doing this occasionally if the wort is poured in immediately after racking is complete. But this should not be done too often, and if it is done, it's better to remove a good deal of the old yeast so that new yeast will have to grow.

Many old books and recipes on both wine and beer making advocate the use of fantastic quantities of yeast—an ounce or even two ounces of dried yeast to the gallon, for instance. Well, if you want to make sure fermentation goes like a bomb, and are terrified that nothing at all will happen, this will make *sure*. It's rather like committing suicide by taking poison, drawing the pin out of a bomb and jumping out of a building at the twentieth floor.

In fact it's preferable always to add *less* yeast than the fermentation needs rather than more. New yeast is the best, cleanest and most vigorous. Add small, though highly active, quantities of yeast and although the fermentation may not start in five minutes, new, clean, vigorous yeast is being formed—and that is the yeast that will take care of the fermentation.

Old yeast dies. Dying, it dissolves in the beer and may be responsible for unpleasant flavours. Some yeast must inevitably die in any fermentation. But if you pour new wort into the entire yeast residue from a previous full fermentation, you are likely to induce mass slaughter of cells and a far greater volume of yeast deposit than usual. In addition, you are leaving in the new beer all the unwanted by-products of the previous fermentation, the things you have racked your beer to eliminate.

Yeast in growing takes up many of the undesirable elements in the wort, things we don't want in the finished beer. This is not only natural, it's logical. The taste for beer is an acquired taste (although it's rather easily acquired). Probably nobody, tasting beer for the very first time, has ever ejaculated loudly and sincerely: 'Nectar of the gods!' Taste for beer is not only an acquired taste, it's a conditioned taste. The beer drinker wants his ale to taste a certain way, and that way is compounded of his beer-drinking experience. Thus if someone came along with a really new beer, slightly or markedly different from the well-known product, it could be glorious stuff and still it wouldn't meet with instant, enthusiastic acceptance.

We therefore want our beer to taste like beer, faults and all. ('My beer, right or wrong.') Consequently, what yeast has always done in beer must continue to be done in beer. And this includes taking up most of the vegetable traces in the wort for yeast nourishment and growth, a process which would be spoiled by supplying so much yeast initially that growth to fermentation point became unnecessary.

The best method is always to prepare, twenty-four or forty-eight hours before fermentation is to start, a fresh yeast starter. This is easily done. First it is necessary to drink two or three pints of beer. If the beer is good, this is no ordeal. Perhaps your friends will help. The sediment from three bottles is shaken up and collected in one of the bottles, and a fresh starter is prepared as before, with malt extract, citric acid and water.

Only if beer making is suspended for several months and all the last brew is drunk does it become necessary to buy more yeast.

There are scores of different beer and wine yeasts on the market, and some people like to experiment with many varieties. Many brewers claim that vast differences can be detected in the finished beers made from different yeasts. Personally I find the same standard sedimentary yeast makes excellent mild ale, pale ale, bitter beer, lager and stout.

If you want to experiment, the most convenient way is to use tablets or packet yeast. These keep well and you need use only a tiny quantity each time to make up a fresh starter.

On the type and condition of the yeast at all stages depends the quality of the beer. The principles to be followed are therefore collected and summarized here.

YEAST

Use a good quality sedimentary beer or ale yeast. Avoid ordinary dried yeast, brewer's yeast and baker's yeast.

Always prepare yeast in advance of the fermentation, making about half a pint of strongly fermenting starter.

Never allow yeast to ferment, either in starter or in the fermentation proper, in the total absence of some kind of acid.

Add less yeast than necessary to any fermentation rather than more. Growth of yeast is a desirable process in the wort.

Allow the yeast to settle well before the first racking, and rack again one or two days later. Failure to do this may mean that the beer will never clear satisfactorily.

Bottle only when the beer is virtually dry (totally fermented) and prime for fresh gas. Only tiny residues of yeast are needed for bottle fermentation, a mere film on the bottom of the bottle.

Allow enough time, ten to thirty days, for complete clearing and adequate bottle fermentation before the beer is drunk. Beer drunk too soon, even if gas content is adequate, has a brewing taste—yeasty, malty, sugary—because until the bottle fermentation is complete, the brewing process is not complete either.

If sediments from bottles are kept for later consumption, they should be poured at once into clean screwtop bottles and allowed to mature again. But this is a stingy practice which may be found more trouble than it's worth. Beer which cleared well the first time may not clear well again.

CHAPTER XI

Loose ends

Champagne certainly gives one werry gentlemanly
ideas, but for a continuance, I don't know but
I should prefer mild hale.

R. S. SURTEES, *Jorrocks's Jaunts and Jollities*

It's one thing to read or be told how to do a thing. It's another when you actually start. There are things you knew all the time and didn't have to be told about at all. And there are other things large and small which have been taken for granted. . . .

When tea was introduced to Britain in the seventeenth century, one lady carefully put the correct quantity of tea in the right sort of container and poured in boiling water. Then she poured away the liquid and ate the tea leaves. She didn't like them. She decided, logically enough, she didn't like tea.

Now whether this is a true story or not, it's a significant story. After all, when you boil an egg you don't throw away the egg and drink the water, do you?

There are many such things which can happen in beer making, and it is for this reason that this book has been based rather on general than on particular methods. If you understand the process, the details will take care of themselves. If you don't understand the process, a small slip in detail can ruin the whole thing.

A certain wine maker (who should certainly have known better) made beer occasionally, and his method included an error as basic as that of the lady who threw away the tea and ate the leaves. In wine making it's common practice to pour boiling water over the fruit to kill unwanted bacteria. So he invariably put his malt in a crock and covered it with boiling water. Thereafter he proceeded by the book. But, of course, he had started by killing the malt's capacity for conversion. He got scarcely more out of his malt than he would have done out of ordinary wheat or barley.

Your own experience is far more valuable than anything I or anyone else can tell you. Don't throw it away.

At least in the case of the first twenty brews, write down everything that is done. Experiment by all means, but remember an experiment is useless and pointless unless an accurate record of it is kept. When you drink your own beer, you should have available a complete record of how it was produced. Then you can do it again.

There will be failures, inevitably. With luck, they will never be total failures. (My only total failure was with a brew, frankly experimental, made with cod-liver oil malt extract.) Remember, however, that although trial and error is an excellent method of learning, it fails utterly unless the error can be pinpointed. This is where records come in. You can't be certain that the one innovation in a particular brew was solely responsible for disappointing results, but it's a reasonable assumption, a working hypothesis. This is why, as in all scientific work, all intelligent experimentation, two variables are never introduced simultaneously. If something goes wrong, which was responsible?

When the home brewer is well past the tyro stage, he can still, with a little thought, improve his beer and produce it more easily. This does not mean that the moment an idea strikes him he turns everything upside down to try it out. Nor does it mean that some new process he reads about should be enthusiastically adopted as the answer to all possible problems. Rather, he should always have an eye to short cuts which aren't going to make the journey longer in the end, and alternative methods which are simpler, quicker, or more efficient than the current ones.

The commercial brewery, for instance, used to be a tall, thin building rather than a short and fat one. Why? Because then gravity, which is always with us, could be made to do half the work. It was easy to lift malt on a hoist to the top of the building, and pipe water there. Since brewing is a series of processes carried out on a liquid, the liquid in question could be run down from floor to floor in a kind of natural production line.

This is no longer necessary, but the home brewer should think along similar lines, not confined to gravity either. If space is restricted, how can it best be used? If space is unlimited, there are probably snags about the kind of space, yet there must be ways of taking advantage of it. A damp cellar useless for most purposes can be used for brewing and storing, with proper safeguards.

Beer in bottles stored to mature on a concrete floor may take up to five times as long as beer bottles standing on wood, especially when the temperature is low anyway. But suppose you want to store for a long time? The best lager owes its particular qualities to being stored for a long time at low temperatures.

Therefore, if you're in a hurry for beer of any kind to mature, store it on something other than a concrete floor in a reasonably high temperature. If you want to make the best lager, or for any other reason want to store a lot of beer without risk either of spoilage or of too vigorous bottle fermentation, store the bottles on a cold concrete floor.

Long experience shows all of us not only the methods we happen to prefer, but also the type of change in those methods which might be worth making.

If a man can build a better mousetrap, though he live in a forest, the world will beat a path to his door. This is still in essence true: what it means as far as the home brewer is concerned is that whenever a better way comes along, he'll find out about it. But he has to be the judge. Is it really a better method, or is it the same old method dressed up, perhaps with a new built-in snag?

When a method works, leave it alone. When it doesn't work, or doesn't work well enough, find out why. The brewer who has learned what to do and why doesn't need a checklist to pinpoint what has gone wrong.

All that is necessary for home brewing to be wholly satisfactory both as a source of cheap beer and as an undemanding hobby is reasonable care and a constantly questioning attitude. Is this the best way, or is there a better way?

Is there a better mousetrap?

CHAPTER XII

Wine

Here's to old Adam's crystal ale,
Clear, sparkling and divine,
Fair H$_2$0 long may you flow,
We drink your health—in wine!

OLIVER HEREFORD, *Toasts*

In *Wine Making for All* I included a chapter on beer. The reason was very simple: basically the processes of making wine and beer are similar, and roughly the same equipment required. There are not very many wine makers who *never* drink beer, or vice versa. I assume teetotallers are no longer with us.

Wine costs scarcely more than beer to make—less, indeed, if you have fruit in your garden and use it.

But the wine maker must take greater care at all stages than the home brewer, and some extra equipment is necessary.

Briefly, this is how wine is made, whether in a Bordeaux château or in a shed behind the gasworks. Juice is pressed or otherwise extracted from fruit. Adjustments are made for taste, sugar content, acidity, tannin, pectin. Yeast is added and the must (not the wort as in beer making) is kept in a container which has a one-way valve providing outlet for gas and no inlet.

This fermentation, unlike that of beer, takes roughly a month, possibly three months. This is why the valve (or fermentation lock) is necessary. If you left beer for from four to thirteen weeks, it would be no great surprise to find it going mouldy. The only thing which prevents wine from going mouldy is the fermentation lock, which allows gas to get out but not in.

Racking of wine is similar to that of beer, but far more racking is necessary. The home brewer *wants* a bottle fermentation; the home wine maker goes to enormous lengths to prevent any such thing, unless he's making champagne.

Now the home brewer, knowing all about bottle fermentation, is liable to champ at the bit at this very idea, and make up his mind on the spot: *I'm going to make champagne*.

Genuine champagne is a very delicate drink. It has not attained its reputation for nothing, although the fact that it has such a reputation has not only inflated the price but also ensured that most champagne is drunk by the wrong people— those who order it *because* it is the most expensive thing to drink (other than spirits), whether they really appreciate it or not. Hollywood is responsible for about half of this adulation of champagne: in thousands of films made between 1920 and 1950, no big celebration scene was complete without some idiot shouting 'Champagne!' Come to think of it, Hollywood hasn't paid off all these idiots yet. The impression hammered home was that when you really want to paint the town red, on any once-in-a-lifetime occasion when nothing is going to stop you having the best, you simply must have champagne. The tough guy comes into the speakeasy and snarls : 'Rye.' The fat, hairy, unwashed truck driver staggers in and demands beer. The plump American millionaire always says : 'Scatch on the racks.' This is characterization. But all this time, anybody good or bad, young or old, male or female, who really wants to *live*, has to have champagne. What else is there?

Champagne is good, but not that good. Among connoisseurs there exists a certain inverted snobbery about champagne. They at least know there are other drinks, and that why champagne costs so much is because it is expensive to produce and not because it is *better* than, say, a Bordeaux château red or a great hock.

Anyway, the champagne produced at home, which is merely an immature wine bottled too soon, can't begin to compare with real champagne, and even that isn't as wonderful as is generally believed. On the other hand, a plum wine made at home, a bramble or fig or apricot wine, really can compare with the greatest French and German grape wines and not suffer by the comparison.

Racking is therefore a long and patient process, designed to make sure that all yeast has been removed and further fermentation is impossible. Wine is racked four, five, six times, every three months, before bottling. Yet the maturing process is far more than this, far more than merely assurance of stability. Long maturing, particularly in oak, can turn a moderate wine into a good one, and a good wine into a great one.

The wine is then bottled, preferably in 26-ounce wine bottles, and stoppered with straight corks (a corking machine is necessary). Unlike screwtop beer bottles, wine bottles are best stored either at an angle or flat on their sides, so that the cork cannot dry out completely, shrink, become a poor seal and allow the wine to spoil.

˙ The length of time wine should be kept depends on its type and strength. It should not be less than a year and in general not more than five. It is a dangerous myth that wine constantly and steadily improves with the passing years, and a fatuous delusion that it gets stronger with age. How could it get stronger? Beer does, in maturing, because beer is primed, there is yeast in the bottle and further fermentation takes place. Wine does not, because by the time dry wines go into the bottle there's no more sugar to ferment anyway, and sweet wines are even more carefully racked to ensure that when they're bottled all yeast has been eliminated. In any case, when a bottle untouched for four or five years is opened, and the wine is clear and still as it should be, that settles it—there has been no bottle fermentation and the wine is of exactly the same alcoholic strength as it was when the cork was inserted.

Wines light in nature and taste, dry, not too fruity wines made from things like rhubarb, gooseberries and grapes, sometimes need no more than a year of maturing, and can actually begin to deteriorate after four or five years. Study of current wine lists will show that the Moselle wines now being offered are usually not more than three years old. Bordeaux wines, on the other hand, may be ten or more years old. The home wine maker *must* keep certain wines like beetroot, sloe and other heavily flavoured wines for at least five years before the taste mellows.

For the home brewer, wine makes unusual demands on his patience. No beer except a fine lager, from the moment of mashing, needs more than a month or so before it can fairly be tasted as a finished product. No wine needs less than a year.

WINE

But there is no harm in making a gallon or two, on the strict understanding with oneself that this is something Not to be Opened until the Christmas after Next.

Wine making is easier than brewing in many ways, although paradoxically far more care is necessary. With grapes, after all, all that is absolutely essential is to crush the grapes, run the juice into a barrel, bung it up and leave it, occasionally knocking out a spile to allow the gas to escape and hammering it back in again. And in the case of other fruits, more acid and less sweet than grapes, water and sugar are added mainly to reduce the acid and increase the sugar, the rest of the process being almost as simple.

Yet beer seldom spoils and wine often does.

If it were possible to explain all that the home wine maker needs to know in a few pages, I shouldn't have written a complete book on it. However, here are some general indications of how to go about it, perhaps adequate for anyone who knows all about the cognate process of making beer.

For a gallon of wine 2–6 lb. of fruit is needed, plus, depending on the fruit and the kind of wine aimed at, anything from 2lb. to 4lb. of sugar, plus the right kind of wine yeast. Beer yeast simply won't do. It would try to produce beer from grapes, plums or blackcurrants, and if this has been a good idea somebody would have done it long ago and become a millionaire.

First a yeast starter is prepared from the right yeast, a sedimentary wine yeast (this is no problem, because *all* wine yeasts are sedimentary), very much as a beer starter is prepared. Indeed, it can be done exactly the same way, with

116

malt extract and a little citric acid. The main difference is that wine yeast works more slowly, steadily, and far longer, and won't grow as quickly as beer yeast or be as violent in the starter bottle. Another thing to bear in mind is that although half a pint of violently active beer yeast is desirable to start a five-gallon beer fermentation, only an ounce or so of not particularly violent wine starter, well diluted, is needed for a gallon of wine. We expect beer fermentations to start almost instantly, and make sure they do. Must in a gallon jar protected at all times by a fermentation lock needn't start fermenting for days, and generally doesn't.

In case anybody's interested, ale yeast is *saccharomyces cerevisiae* and wine yeast *saccharomyces ellipsoideus*.

When the yeast starter is ready, an extract is prepared from the fruit. There is nothing in wine making comparable to mashing. All that is necessary is a method of extracting as much juice as possible from the fruit without carrying forward too many solids. The many methods recommended are all compromises. Boil and you get more or less everything. Use cold water throughout and you get more or less nothing. So the commonest compromise is to pour boiling water over clean fruit, leave it until cool and then squeeze the softened fruit to extract as much as possible.

Wine makers use a safeguard unnecessary in beer making, Campden tablets, to kill off unwanted bacteria which may have survived even the soaking in boiling water. Campden tablets, obtainable from chemists for jam making and fruit preserving, contain sulphur dioxide, which is a preservative— and a poison. If your local butcher puts too much sulphur dioxide in his sausages, he will be taken to court and fined. Obviously, Campden tablets must be used with care.

Sugar, as we know very well, should always be dissolved in the wort before yeast is added, but a little can be added dry as priming in bottles. This, however, is when beer yeast is used. Wine yeast is less vigorous. Sugar should never be added direct in wine making. It should always be added in the form of syrup, sugar dissolved in water and then cooled.

The strained fruit juice, probably only a couple of pints or so, is poured into a gallon jar. One or at most two Campden tablets are dissolved in the juice, and the syrup is added. Acid is probably not necessary, since there are few fruits wholly lacking in acid, and most have too much. Only if imported dried fruit is used, such as dates, figs or apricots, must acid be added. Our old friend citric will do very well, about half an ounce to the gallon, although an experienced wine maker may have good reasons for including tartaric or malic acid, or both. Yeast nutrient, dismissed curtly earlier in beer making, is desirable if not obligatory in wine making. Tannin is always useful, sometimes essential. The must is made up with water, the active wine yeast is added, and the fermentation lock fitted.

All being well, nothing more need be done for about a month.

The hydrometer is more necessary in wine making than in brewing. The experienced brewer can leave his hydrometer in its box for months on end, knowing by other observations the state of his wort or beer. But the wine maker should take hydrometer readings at certain stages as a matter of course.

Wine is a stronger drink than beer, and is treated as such. Wine is drunk in small glasses. Even the lightest wines are stronger, volume for volume, than any but the most powerful beers.

In wine, as in beer, the potential strength is determined by the initial hydrometer reading. A weak beer ferments to zero from an initial gravity of less than 30. Average beers are in the range 30–50. Very strong beers begin to ferment at about 80.

Wine with an initial S.G. of 80 would be considered very light. It is such wines which 'don't travel'. They can be very pleasant drunk in their own district of France, Germany, Austria, Italy, Yugoslavia or Hungary, but if they are exported and shaken about in transport they can be disappointing. Usually, in consequence, they are not exported.

An ordinary dry wine has an initial S.G. of 100. Over 120, wines are liable not to ferment to zero. A certain unfermented residue remains in them and they turn out sweet wines. If the initial S.G. is still higher, 130–170, the finished wine is bound to be sweet.

The amateur wine maker therefore uses the hydrometer to determine the kind of wine he means to produce. Records are more necessary for him; without them he would never have a clue about what was going on. And in wine making it's absolutely necessary to know what's going on. Once a beer fermentation is properly started, nothing short of an abrupt drop in temperature to zero or below is likely to halt it. Although we check before bottling to make sure the S.G. is low enough, we seldom find that the fermentation has hung up at, say, 15 or 20. If the S.G. is 15 or 20, all that's needed is a little patience. Wine, on the other hand, frequently sticks for no obvious reason. Must originally 100 can quite easily ferment normally to about 40 (or almost any other figure) and then mulishly stop. Patience is not enough; the wine may stick at 40 indefinitely. The wine maker, having established by taking hydrometer readings for several days running that the fermentation is well and truly stuck, must take steps to unstick it —put the jar in a warmer room, shake it, add yeast nutrient, citric acid or Vitamin B tablets, or pour it into another jar to aerate it. Failure to ensure that the S.G. drops eventually to the expected level before bottling would result in something similar to the catastrophe of bottling beer too soon, except that it would take longer. Next spring, when the temperature rose, yeast would grow and start a bottle fermentation. Corks would grow and start a bottle fermentation. Corks would fly and bottles burst. . . .

It cannot be too strongly emphasized that wine, compared with beer, is delicate and sickly, a shy virgin that must be guarded against the evils of the world.

Beer doesn't need a fermentation lock; wine does. Even after racking, beer can take care of itself, and even kept in bottles only half full it probably won't spoil.

Wine, especially after the first racking, should always be kept in jars or bottles with as little air space as possible at the top. So long as fermentation is going on at all, this isn't absolutely vital, since some carbon dioxide is still being released and protective pressure will be maintained. But later, even a fermentation lock can't afford full protection. Eventually the wine will begin to suck air in instead of blowing it out. And if a plain stopper is fitted, fermentation being complete, only a tiny air space should be left. A gap of even an inch or two can lead to the destruction of the wine.

The same applies when the wine is eventually bottled.

WINE

Dark bottles must be used for red wine, since light affects the colour. In the case of beer I strongly recommended clear bottles because the convenience of being able to watch the yeast while pouring far outweighs any adverse effect that clear glass might have on colour. Besides, beer colour is not nearly as important as that of red wine, and the beer isn't in the bottles very long anyway. Wine, on the other hand, may be in the bottles for years.

The beer maker who wants to make wine as an experiment won't need any more information than has been given here. If he wants to do it as rather more than a mere experiment, he should read at least one of the many detailed books on the subject. Modesty forbids me even to hint at the one I think he should consult.

Anyway, even the perfectly satisfied home brewer would be well advised to make a little wine. Even if he prefers beer, he is bound to have guests who don't. And it is pleasant always to have in the house a small stock of wine which has cost virtually nothing to produce.

> *For why*
> *Should every creature drink but I,*
> *Why, man of morals, tell me why?*
>
> ABRAHAM COWLEY

Appendix

Items mentioned in the text—malt, malt extract, hops, hop extract, all other ingredients, jars, tap jars, casks, siphons, fermentation locks and all wine-making materials—can be obtained from any of the following suppliers:

> Leigh-Williams & Sons,
> Tattenhall, Near Chester.

> Semplex Home Brews Ltd.,
> Old Hall Works,
> Stuart Road, Birkenhead.

> W. R. Loftus Ltd.
> 1–3 Charlotte Street,
> London W.1.

This is by no means a comprehensive list, but each of the three suppliers above seems able to offer important and valu-

APPENDIX

able items either unobtainable or difficult to obtain elsewhere.
All can supply comprehensive catalogues.

For cheap malt extract in bulk:

> Edme Ltd.,
> 120 Regent Street,
> London W.1.

A monthly magazine on wine making which also devotes a
fair amount of space to home brewing is:

> The Amateur Winemaker,
> North Croye, The Avenue,
> Andover, Hants.

Requiem

I drink for the thirst to come.

FRANÇOIS RABELAIS

Index

125

INDEX